J. K. STEI

The Collected Works of a Victorian poet

This, the first edition, is limited to
Two Hundred and Fifty copies.

This is No. 104

Compiled and edited by D. J. Leighton

First published in Great Britain in February 2008 by
Hydrangea Publishing,
6 Walnut Tree Cottages,
London
SW19 5DN

ISBN 978-0-9548495-1-1

A catalogue record of this book is available
from the British Library.

Printed by Intype Libra, Elm Grove, Wimbledon, SW19 4HE

Typeset by GR Typesetting, Cambridge, UK

Front Cover:
A chalk drawing of James Kenneth Stephen
by Frederick Miller dated 1887, and used by Stephen
in his Lapsus Calami book of verse.

James Kenneth Stephen lived from 1859–1892 and is regarded as one of the most talented creators of parodies and light verse of the 19th century. Educated at Eton, and King's College, Cambridge, he was for a while the tutor to the Duke of Clarence, the eldest grandson of Queen Victoria, and second in line to the throne. Virginia Woolf was his cousin. To this day there is a suspicion that he may have been involved in the 'Jack the Ripper' murders in London's East End.

Stephen qualified as a barrister, but his real love was literature and poetry. His verses were published in many respected magazines such as *The Pall Mall Gazette*, *The Cambridge Review*, *The Spectator*, *The St. James's Gazette* and *The Globe*. In 1888 he started his own magazine *The Reflector* and this too carried many of his poems. Most notably, he published two slim volumes of his work, *Lapsus Calami* and *Quo Musa Tendis?*, both of which were reprinted.

Unfortunately, throughout his life he was subject to extremes of enthusiasm and depression, which led to erratic behaviour. He was expelled from London's Savile Club for aggression, and was briefly imprisoned in Paris for fraud. Eventually his health declined, and he died aged 32 in an asylum. The quality of his poetry was recognised at the time, and has continued to be held in high regard. This is the first time that a comprehensive collection of his work has been published.

To Robert
With best wishes

John Leighton.

D. J. Leighton was educated at King's College School, Wimbledon and later at Christ's Hospital. On leaving school he became a salesman with Unilever, and later spent time in advertising and the Middle East. He is now retired, and lives in Wimbledon with his wife Ann.

He is a member of the Poetry Society.

Contents

'After'

'To'

After Sunset

1. Aug. 30, 1891 – At Magna Charta Island

A grey lawn cut by the river's brink,
   And then the stream,
Dun slabs of marble, splashed with ink,
   Beyond—a dream!—
A purple shield of blazing bronze
   Streaked here and there with silver: a pair
Of rainbow-coloured swans.

And above the blaze of the burnished river
   The burnished sky,
Bronze banners of vapour which hardly quiver
   As the breeze goes by,
Girt round with a dark blue belt of cloud;
   One primrose patch, which the ripples catch,
And the first of the stars' blithe crowd.

And between the water and sky one observes
   A slope, tree-crowned:
Black tree-tops tracing a thousand curves,
   Where gloom's profound;
And grey-green meadows from slope to stream,
   With a steep black bank at the edge: how thank
The fate which allows man's brain to house
   Such a spirit-soothing dream.

2. *Sept. 5, 1891 – In the Lock-Cut: Old Windsor*

Great purple clouds in the western sky,
    Hung thick o'er a blaze of golden white,
And below that glory there seems to lie,
    A cushion of silver: not so bright
But it dulls to a grey that entombs the day
    And heralds the march of night.

One tree hides a third of the gorgeous west,—
    A disk of black is its dusky growth—
Yet not hides: nay perhaps displays at best
    Through the chinks which it opens, nothing loth:
While its outline bold cuts silver and gold,
    And heightens the blaze of both.

And up to the glory of golden white,
    With the purple above and the silver below,
There's a river lane that is darkly bright,
    Softly and smoothly and quietly aglow,
Blue willows beside it, night hasting to hide it,
    Day sorry to let it go.

The tree grows blacker, the night falls fast,
    And purple and silver and white must fade:
But something was shown us which can't but last:
    Has a song been sung? has a play been played?
Has a lesson been taught, or was all for naught?
    Well—nothing endures like the past.

3. Sept. 9, 1891 – Off the Bells of Ouseley

The Poet
The water is black and opaque and polished,
    Not a ripple to break it, or ray to illume:
From bank to bank, like the sunless tank,
    Swept clear of ripples by some witch-broom:
What's it like, dear Muse? come! impart your views,
    Or, faith, you'll be soon abolished.

The Muse
Just the dripping asphalte of rain-washed Paris,
    With our gliding punt for the rumbling tram;
And your face shining black in the glistening track:
    On the bank, for the workman who drains his dram,
One willow as grim as a phantom dim
    Evoked by Augustus Harris.

After the Golden Wedding

(*Three Soliloquies*)

1. The husband's
She's not a faultless woman; no!
  She's not an angel in disguise:
She has her rivals here below:
  She's not an unexampled prize:

She does not always see the point
  Of little jests her husband makes:
And, when the world is out of joint,
  She makes a hundred small mistakes:

She's not a miracle of tact:
  Her temper's not the best I know:
She's got her little faults in fact,
  Although I never tell her so.

But this, my wife, is why I hold you
  As good a wife as ever stepped,
And why I meant it when I told you
  How cordially our feast I kept:

You've lived with me these fifty years,
  And all the time you loved me dearly:
I may have given you cause for tears:
  I may have acted rather queerly.

I ceased to love you long ago:
    I loved another for a season:
As time went on I came to know
    Your worth, my wife: and saw the reason

Why such a wife as you have been
    Is more than worth the world beside;
You loved me all the time, my Queen;
    You couldn't help it if you tried.

You loved me as I once loved you,
    As each loved each beside the altar:
And whatsoever I might do,
    Your loyal heart could never falter.

And, if you sometimes fail me, sweetest,
    And don't appreciate me, dear,
No matter: such defects are meetest
    For poor humanity, I fear.

And all's forgiven, all's forgot,
    On this our golden wedding day;
For, see! she loves me: does she not?
    So let the world e'en go its way.

I'm old and nearly useless now,
    Each day a greater weakling proves me:
There's compensation anyhow:
    I still possess a wife that loves me.

2. The wife's
Dear worthy husband! good old man!
   Fit hero of a golden marriage:
I'll show towards you, if I can,
   An absolutely wifely carriage.

The months or years which your career
   May still comprise before you perish,
Shall serve to prove that I, my dear,
   Can honour, and obey, and cherish.

Till death us part, as soon he must,
   (And you, my dear, should shew the way)
I hope you'll always find me just
   The same as on our wedding day.

I never loved you, dearest: never!
   Let that be clearly understood:
I thought you good, and rather clever,
   And found you really rather good.

And, what was more, I loved another,
   But couldn't get him: well, but, then
You're just as bad, my erring brother,
   You most impeccable of men:—

Except for this: my love was married
 Some weeks before I married you:
While you, my amorous dawdler, tarried
 Till we'd been wed a year or two.

You loved me at our wedding: I
 Loved some one else: and after that
I never cast a loving eye
 On others: you—well, tit for tat!

But after all I made you cheerful:
 Your whims I've humoured: saw the point
Of all your jokes: grew duly tearful,
 When you were sad, yet chose the joint

You liked the best of all for dinner,
 And soothed you in your hours of woe:
Although a miserable sinner,
 I *am* a good wife, as wives go.

I bore with you and took your side,
 And kept my temper all the time:
I never flirted; never cried,
 Nor ranked it as a heinous crime,

When you preferred another lady,
 Or used improper words to me,
Or told a story more than shady,
 Or snored and snorted after tea,

Or otherwise gave proofs of being
    A dull and rather vain old man:
I still succeeded in agreeing
    With all you said, (the safest plan),

Yet always strove my point to carry,
    And make you do as I desired:
I'm *glad* my people made me marry!
    They hit on just what I required.

Had love been wanted—well, I couldn't
    Have given what I'd not to give;
Or had a genius asked me! wouldn't
    The man have suffered? now, we live

Among our estimable neighbours
    A decent and decorous life:
I've earned by my protracted labours
    The title of a model wife.

But when beneath the turf you're sleeping,
    And I am sitting here in black,
Engaged, as they'll suppose, in weeping,
    I shall not wish to have you back.

3. The Vicar's
A good old couple! kind and wise!
   And oh! what love for one another!
They've won, those two, life's highest prize,
   Oh! let us copy them, my brother.

After Walt Whitman

The clear cool note of the cuckoo which has ousted
   the legitimate nest-holder,
The whistle of the railway guard despatching the
   train to the inevitable collision,
The maiden's monosyllabic reply to a polysyllabic
   proposal,
The fundamental note of the last trump, which is
   presumably D natural;
All of these are sounds to rejoice in, yea to let
   your very ribs re-echo with:
But better than all of them is the absolutely last
   chord of the apparently inexhaustible pianoforte
   player.

A Grievance

after Lord George Byron

Dear Mr Editor: I wish to say—
    If you will not be angry at my writing it—
But I've been used, since childhood's happy day,
    When I have thought of something, to inditing it:
I seldom think of things: and, by the way,
    Although this metre may not be exciting, it
Enables one to be extremely terse,
Which is not what one always is in verse.

I used to know a man,—such things befall
    The observant wayfarer through Fate's domain:
He was a man, take him for all in all,
    We shall not look upon his like again:
I know that statement's not original:
    What statement is, since Shakspere? or, since Cain,
What murder? I believe 'twas Shakspere said it, or
Perhaps it may have been your Fighting Editor.

Though why an Editor should fight, or why
    A Fighter should abase himself to edit,
Are problems far too difficult and high
    For me to solve with any sort of credit:
Some greatly more accomplished man than I
    Must tackle them: let's say then Shakspere said it:
And, if he did not, Lewis Morris may
(Or even if he did). Some other day,

When I have nothing pressing to impart,
    I should not mind dilating on this matter:
I feel its import both in head and heart,
    And always did,—especially the latter:
I could discuss it in the busy mart
    Or on the lonely housetop: hold! this chatter
Diverts me from my purpose. To the point:
The time, as Hamlet said, is out of joint,

And I perhaps was born to set it right;
    A fact I greet with perfect equanimity;
I do not put it down to "cursed spite":
    I don't see any cause for cursing in it: I
Have always taken very great delight
    In such pursuits since first I read divinity:
Whoever will may write a nation's songs
As long as I'm allowed to right its wrongs.

What's Eton but a nursery of wrong-righters,
    A mighty mother of effective men,
A training-ground for amateur reciters,
    A sharpener of the sword as of the pen,
A factory of orators and fighters,
    A forcing-house of genius? Now and then,
The world at large shrinks back, abashed and beaten,
Unable to endure the glare of Eton.

I think I said I knew a man: what then?
   I don't suppose such knowledge is forbid:
We nearly all do, more or less, know men,—
   Or think we do: nor will a man get rid
Of that delusion, while he wields a pen:
   But who this man was, what, if aught, he did,
Nor why I mentioned him, I do not know:
Nor what I "wished to say" a while ago.

A Joke

You cannot, will not, never could;
Of course I knew it, what's the good?
I know you, you know me, and then
You know so many other men:
You like them all, you like me too;
And most of them in love with you!

But if it had been otherwise:
If I had happened, in your eyes,
To be what other men have been
In other people's eyes, my queen:
Why then, why then,—confound it all,
The world's abominably small!
I mean the world of sense and feeling;
A truism there's no concealing.

You're smiling: as you smiled before,
While I was asking you for more
Than you could give me, when I chanced
To drop a jest, how quick you glanced!
You seemed to say that love (we use
The word; how not?) would scarcely choose
Such phrases as we jesters store,
To "set the table in a roar."

Ah! if you'd wanted words red hot,
You might have had them; you did not,
It's hardly decent, I opine,
To prate of beautiful, divine,
Describe one's amorous symptoms, gloat
On eyes, and hands, and hair, and throat,
And magnify one's lady's charms,
Like Troubadour or knight at arms,
Unless one has the luck to know
That she would rather have it so.
Faint heart—I know: I'm not the man
To do it, though my betters can,
Suffice it all the words are there
To thrill the circumambient air,
The moment I'm allowed: meanwhile
Why not encourage you to smile:
Relieve the tedium of a scene
You're used to? since I do not mean
To veil my eyes or bow my head,
Or weep, or wish that I were dead,
Or fail to fight the fight of life,
As keenly as were you my wife.
You're smiling still: you don't believe
A hopeless lover would not grieve;
A grieving lover would not show
Some outward token of his woe:
I'm joking, am I? be it so.

An Afterthought

The good a man does from time to time,
   Gets thanks and praise for, is crowned with bays for
Or married for, sung for in verse sublime,
Or placed for in marble in civic halls
Or hung for in oils on palace walls:

Is good that deserves to be hymned, no doubt,
   Commemorated, and duly fêted,
And otherwise made much noise about:
And of course it is well that the men are found,
To do such good, and to be so crowned.

But all the good that was ever done,
   Or even tried for, or longed or sighed for,
By all the great men under the sun,
Since men were invented, or genius glowed,
Or the world was furnished for our abode:

Is worth far less than the merest smile,
   Or touch of finger, or sighs that linger,
When cheeks grow dimpled, and lips lack guile,
On the face of the women whom God gives grace
To—well on a certain woman's face.

An Election Address

(To Cambridge University, 1882)

I venture to suggest that I
    Am rather noticeably fit
To hold the seat illumined by
    The names of Palmerston and Pitt.

My principles are such as you
    Have often heard expressed before:
They are, without exception, true;
    And who can say, with candour, more?

My views concerning Church and State
    Are such as Bishops have professed:
I need not recapitulate
    The arguments on which they rest.

Respecting Ireland, I opine
    That Ministers are in a mess,
That Landlords rule by Right Divine,
    That Firmness will remove Distress.

I see with horror undisguised
    That freedom of debate is dead:
The Liberals are organised:
    The Caucus rears its hideous head.

Yet need'st thou, England, not despair
　　At Chamberlain's or Gladstone's pride,
While Henry Cecil Raikes is there
　　To organise the other side.

I never quit, as others do,
　　Political intrigue, to seek
The dingy literary crew,
　　Or hear the voice of science speak.

But I have fostered, guided, planned
　　Commercial enterprise: in me
Some ten or twelve directors and
　　Six worthy chairmen you may see.

My academical career
　　Was free from any sort of blot:
I challenge anybody here
　　To demonstrate that it was not.

At classics too I worked amain,
　　Whereby I did not only pass,
But even managed to obtain
　　A very decent second class.

And since those early days, the same
　　Success has crowned the self-same plan;
Profundity I cannot claim:
　　Respectability I can.

An Election Address, Dec. 1890

(Air: *The Wearing of the Green*)

Kilkenny dear, and did ye hear this most surprising
news?
Here's three bould men come coortin' you and which
can you refuse?
A bigger and a bloodier fight has never yet been seen,
And they're breaking one another's heads in
Committee Room fifteen.

I met Chief Justice Healy and I took him by the hand:
"Oh! how is ould Ireland, and how does she stand?"
Potatoes rot and peasants pine: disthress will soon
be seen:
And they're breaking one another's heads in
Committee Room fifteen."

Dear Dillon and O'Brien bould, as I have heard
men tell,
Have gone to North Amerikey, their resources for
to swell;
But they're coming back to prison and the try-your-
weight machine,
And to break the other fellows' heads in Committee
Room fifteen.

There's *Disunited Ireland* (but that same has been
    suppressed):
There's some "cowardly little scoundrels" and a nicely
    feathered nest;
There's lots of cash in Paris, and the wigs are on the
    green,
And they're breaking one another's heads in
    Committee Room fifteen.

There's bloody Arthur Balfour, that priest-destroying
    man,
'Tis he that passed Coercion, and does all the harm
    he can,
A blacker and a baser brute there never yet has been,
And he chuckles o'er the broken heads in Committee
    Room fifteen.

He gets upon an outside car,—'tis he that has the
    power—
Goes up and down the land and seeks for what we
    may devour—
And bedad we're glad to see him, and 'tis he likes
    being seen,
And they're breaking one another's heads in
    Committee Room fifteen.

And here is Mr S......., and who the deuce is he?
And what's he after doing, and why would he be M.P.?
For he first says "God save Ireland!" and then "God
    save the Queen!"
And he blackguards thim bould fighting bhoys in
    Committee Room fifteen.

A Pair of Fools

1. *His account of the matter*

I met you dear, I met you: I can't be robbed of that;
   Despite the crowd, the babble, and the military band;
I met you, yes, I met you: and by your side I sat;
   I looked at you, I talked to you, and twice I held
      your hand.

When you are with me, dearest, the crowd is out of sight;
   The men who smoke, the men who pose, the sharpers,
      and the flats;
The people quite unfit to walk beneath the heaven's light;
   The green and yellow women with intolerable hats.

The sun was bright: the dahlias flashed: the trees, in summer
      sheen,
   Shut out the dusty houses, hushed the turmoil of the
      street;
But, had the charm of peace enhanced the sweetness of the
      scene,
   Even so your beauty had eclipsed the whole of it, my
      sweet.

I talked to you, you listened; I passed from grave to gay,
   With what a world of sympathy you gently murmured
      "Yes!"
A merry "No," a soft "Perhaps," a glance the other way:
   An eyebrow raised, a foot that tapped, a rustle of your
      dress.

You smiled, ah! what a smile is yours; your depth of hazel
eyes
Shook conscious of the thought within, expressed but
unexplained;
Your speaking face that glowed with all a girl's sedate
surprise;
"That brow of hers," as Browning says: the thoughts that it
contained!

I talked as ne'er before; to you my eloquence belonged;
You spoke, dear, with my lips, 'twas I that listened and
approved;
Strange subtle phrases sprang, and thoughts as deep as novel
thronged:
I know you knew, I swear you did, how ardently I loved.

We parted, and you looked at me in silence: and I knew
The meaning of the look: I'll come to-morrow if I live;
To-morrow I shall come, and I will say a word to you,
And you will speak, at last, the words that hope and
rest can give.

2. *Her account of the matter*

I met him in the park my dear; he *is* funny man;
   Impossible to separate his earnest from his fun;
He talks, and talks, it's deadly dull: I smile, you know
     the plan;
   And, when particularly grave, he makes a jest of one,

The park was full of people; Maud had such a lovely dress
   A dream of greeny silk and gauze and primrose ribbons,
     oh!
I wished I had one; and her hat! I tried and tried to guess
   How much it cost; she buys the stuff and makes a hat, you
     know.

I think I sat with him an hour: there *was* a crowd my dear,
   Some pretty girls: one lovely one: and four attractive men:
Old Mrs Robinson was there and Mr Vere de Vere,
   And not another soul I knew: I shall not go again.

I don't know what we talked about: I smiled: the same old
     smile:
   I "yes'd" and "no'd" and "really'd," till I thought he must
     discover
That I was listening to the band: I wondered all the while
   If such a dull old gentleman could ever be a lover.

Perhaps some solemn sober girl with eyes a foot across,
    Smooth neatly-parted hair, no stays, elastic-sided boots,
Will yearn at him and marry him: I shan't regret his loss:
    I really think some kinds of men are lower than the brutes.

He went at last, the prig! He'll come to-morrow if he can,
    He means to recollect our talk—*ours* mind you—all his
        life:
Confound—I beg your pardon, dear—well, bless the little
        man!
    And bless the little woman who becomes his little wife!

3. *My account of the matter*

A pair of fools: the man was vain,
    The woman frivolous, 'tis plain:
And each an egoist in thought:
    One dived for self: the other sought
Self on the surface: fools, you see:
    Two fools. Perhaps there'll soon be three:
For now they're married, he and she.

A Pair of Portraits

1. He

Oh yes! I know the sort of man!
    A not entirely vacant eye:
A ready smile, a kind of style;
    A forehead adequately high:
Curls more or less Olympian.

A fund of common things to say,
    A list of common actions done:
A taste for tea, a poll degree,
    A mild delight in harmless fun:
In short, a rather taking way.

The type is common: wherefore tarry
    To paint what all must know so well?
He's rather tall, his feet are small:
    He's thoroughly conventional:
A man who moves in common grooves,
    A never startles you at all:
Or, all in one sad phrase to tell,
    The sort of man that women marry.

2. She

I know the girl: "divinely fair"
  Of course "and most divinely tall:"
A modest yet a queenly air:
  A voice that's keen but musical:
A mind above the common run,
But soft and kind, when all is done,
    And womanly withal.

A girl who might aspire to light
  A gifted worker's rugged way:
To make the very darkness bright
  With love's illuminating ray:
To kindle some grave rugged man,
With genius, ready, if it can,
    To flash upon the day.

A girl to soothe when days are drear:
  To cheer you on when hope grows dim:
A girl who should not greatly fear,
  For truth, however harsh and grim,
To scorn conventionalities:
The sort of woman, if you please,
    Who marries men like him.

A Paradox?

*To F. C. H.**

(*A Conversation Recapitulated*)

TO FIND OUT WHAT YOU CANNOT DO,
   AND THEN TO GO AND DO IT:
There lies the golden rule: but few
I ever found above the ground,
   Except myself, who knew it.

You bid me do from day to day
   The single thing I can do;
I can't do what I can't, you say?
Indeed I can; why, hang it man!
   I solve it *ambulando.*

I cannot draw the simplest thing:
   I cannot guess a riddle:
I cannot dance, or skate, or sing:
I can't compose, and, goodness knows,
   I cannot play the fiddle.

*Francis Coldwell Holland

And yet, to take a single case,
   Of all an illustration,
At thirty-two (to my disgrace?)
I did begin the violin,
   By way of recreation.

The way to go to work is taught
   By precept and correction;
To do it nearly as you ought
You learn by force of pains,—of course
   I don't suggest perfection.

"But, ah! you can't acquire an ear,
   If Nature don't bestow it:"
Excuse me: try before you sneer:
The pains you take an "ear" will make,
   As practice makes a poet.

The sounds, by Nature's laws, are there;
   And all one's education
Is just to catch them in the air:
Success is due entirely to
   Attentive observation.

"Trained ear: trained fingers,—net result.
   A tenth-rate fiddler." Granted!
Plus hours well spent in patient cult
Of music, which you own is rich
   In gifts not else implanted.

Well! so with all the other things:
  You *can* learn how to do them:
You're born with rudiments of wings:
You'll fly in time, and—end sublime!—
  You get a pleasure through them.

"Ah, well!" you answer, "be it so:
  Although of course it's not so:
You've learned to scrape a fiddle-bow;
And what remains? Your addled brains
  Collapse: men die forgot so!

"You've done the thing you couldn't do:
  You're just a dilettante:
Yes, that's about the truth of you:
You'll end, I'm sure, an amateur,
  A mere pococurante!"

Ah! there, my friend, I *know* you're wrong!
  For what you're best at doing,
Law, painting, science, speech or song,
Is just what you are bound to do,
  Whate'er beside pursuing.

The small pursuits you undertake
  For innocent diversion,
No earthly difference will make:
The work goes on till life be gone:
  I stand by that assertion!

Although a modest man, my friend,
   I'll make you this confession:
I feel that I have got an "End"—
A *telos*, eh? as you would say—
   My *métier*, my profession:

Which is—: well, never mind the name;
   But, Frank, I do assure you,
Whatever other little game
I chance to play from day to day—
   (I hope I do not bore you?

I'm aiming at a certain chat
   I had with you, and therefore
You *must* attend, my worthy friend)—
Will not effect the least neglect
   Of what I really care for.

A Parodist's Apology

If I've dared to laugh at you, Robert Browning,
    'Tis with eyes that with you have often wept:
You have oftener left me smiling or frowning,
    Than any beside, one bard except.

But once you spoke to me, storm-tongued poet,
    A trivial word in an idle hour;
But thrice I looked on your face and the glow it:
    Bore from the flame of the inward power.

But you'd many a friend you never knew of,
    Your words lie hid in a hundred hearts,
And thousands of hands that you've grasped but few of
    Would be raised to shield you from slander's darts.

For you lived in the sight of the land that owned you,
    You faced the trial, and stood the test:
They have piled you a cairn that would fain have stoned
        you:
    You have spoken your message and earned your rest.

A Political Allegory

Once there was a famous nation
    With a long and glorious past:
Very splendid was its station,
    And its territory vast:
It had won the approbation,
The applause and admiration,
Of the states who'd had occasion,
In a time of tribulation,
And of disorganisation,
Not to mention degradation,
And profound humiliation,
    To observe it standing fast
Without any trepidation,
Or a sign of vacillation,
    Firm and faithful to the last.

Came a time of dire distraction,
    Full of terror and despair,
When a delicate transaction
    Called for unexampled care;
But the people were directed,
Both the well and ill-affected,
To a wholly unexpected
And surprising course of action,
    Based on motives new and rare
(Being governed by a faction,
    As they generally were).

In a little time the nation
    Had a chance of saying whether
It and its administration
    Seemed inclined to pull together:
And it spoke its mind with vigour:—
    "Such disgraceful conduct must
Everlastingly disfigure
    Future annals, and disgust
Evermore the candid student:
You have been unwise, imprudent,
    Pusillanimous, unjust,
And neglectful of the glory
    Appertaining to our name
Till this melancholy story
    Put a period to our fame."

So this faction, disappointed,
    Lost the national good graces,
And their rivals were anointed,
    And were set in the high places.

Pretty soon arose conditions
    Most embarrassing and hard,
And the party politicians
    Had to be upon their guard.
Illegitimate ambitions,
Democratic rhetoricians,
Persons prone to base submissions,
Men of warlike dispositions,
Wild and wicked statisticians,

Metaphysical magicians,
People apt to sign petitions,
Men inclined to make conditions,
   And a host of wary foes,
Compassed round the ruling faction:
But a certain line of action
   They incontinently chose:
And with great determination,
And extreme discrimination,
Not untouched by exaltation,
After proper preparation,
And profound examination,
Wrought it out with acclamation,
And each other's approbation,
Till the national taxation
   Not unnaturally rose.

To the nation now occurred an
   Opportunity of saying
What they thought about the burden
   Which the government was laying
On their shoulders: and they said it
   In uncompromising terms:—
"Your behaviour would discredit
   Tigers, crocodiles and worms:

You have ruined and disgraced us,
And successfully effaced us
From the proud commanding station
Where the zeal and penetration
   Of our ancestors had placed us.
Go! we are a ruined nation;
   But before our dissolution
We pronounce your condemnation—
   Sappers of our constitution,
Slayers of our reputation!"

But the nation—mark the moral,
   For its value is untold—
During each successive quarrel
   Grew and prospered as of old.

A Remonstrance

Love is what lacks then: but what does it mean to you?
  Where did you hear of it, feel it, or see?
What has the truth, or the good of it been to you?
  How love some other, yet nohow love me?

If there were any conspicuous fault in me,
  Any defect it were torture to bear,
Low-lying levels, too deep to exalt, in me,
  Dread possibilities in me to fear:

If I were ugly or old or untractable,
  Mean in my methods or low in my views:
If I were dull or unpleasant: in fact able
  Neither to please, nor elate, nor amuse:—

That makes you angry, impatient; we'll take it, then,
  I am a man that to know 's to esteem:
That's the admission you make to me: make it then:
  Well why not love me? what's love but a dream?

Only of course in the sense you bestow on it:
  I have a meaning for love, that is plain:
Further than passion, and longing, and so on, it
  Means to me liking and liking again:

Liking and liking, and liking—that's plain enough;—
  Something depending on qualities then?
Yes, for they give you both pleasure and pain enough,
  Qualities common in women and men.

Still not a doubt that, the love being brought about,
  Liking made love, there is more that will come:
All the good qualities ever yet thought about:—
  Yes they fall short of that excellent sum.

Like a man: like him: and let there be more of it
  That which he is he'll be liked for: at last
Love in a minute will flash—I am sure of it—
  Whether the wedding be future or past.

You who consider it quite immaterial
  Whether the person is worthy or not:
You who are looking for something ethereal,
  Something celestrial, transcending our lot:

You to whom every excellent quality
  Means but a cypher: who hope to behold
Love at a burst in his mighty totality
  Change all the grey of the world into gold:

You deam a priceless love: I feel a penny one:
  My reason plods, while your fancy can range:—
Therefore I ask, since you'll never love any one,
  Why should you not marry me for a change?

A Sonnet

Two voices are there: one is of the deep;
It learns the storm-cloud's thunderous melody,
Now roars, now murmurs with the changing sea,
Now bird-like pipes, now closes soft in sleep:
And one is of an old half-witted sheep
Which bleats articulate monotony,
And indicates that two and one are three,
That grass is green, lakes damp, and mountains steep:
And, Wordsworth, both are thine: at certain times
Forth from the heart of thy melodious rhymes,
The form and pressure of high thoughts will burst:
At other times—good Lord! I'd rather be
Quite unacquainted with the A. B. C.
Than write such hopeless rubbish as thy worst.

A Thought

If all the harm that women have done
Were put in a bundle and rolled into one,
   Earth would not hold it,
   The sky could not enfold it,
It could not be lighted nor warmed by the sun;
   Such masses of evil
   Would puzzle the devil
And keep him in fuel while Time's wheels run.

But if all the harm that's been done by men
Were doubled and doubled and doubled again,
And melted and fused into vapour and then
Were squared and raised to the power of ten,
There wouldn't be nearly enough, not near,
To keep a small girl for the tenth of a year.

A Triolet

Is a grand but eccentric old man
    To be found in this commonplace year?
Mr. ——, deny it who can,
Is a grand but eccentric old man.
No age, since the ages began,
    Was so dull as the present; but here
Is a grand but eccentric old man
    To be found in this commonplace year.

Autumn Thoughts

Winter in the College Garden,
  Twigs for leaves, and snow for grass,
Biting blasts that sear and harden
  Where soft zephyrs used to pass,
Hidden places, white bare spaces;—
  What a change it was!

Months have passed since I beheld it:
  Soon it may be here again,
Summer's gone: grey ghosts expelled it:
  Sad's the murmur of the rain:—
"Winter, winter!"—dreary hinter:
  Hear the dull refrain.

As I sit this wet October
  Russet leaf-clouds whirling by,
Can I but be grave and sober,
  Drooping spirit, downcast eye,
Thinking dimly, brooding grimly;—
  Winter, winter's nigh?

And the world that I'm recalling:—
  Such a world of burnished snow!
Scarce a brown leaf left for falling:
  Not a green leaf left to show
How the splendid colours blended
  Twenty weeks ago!

Up and down the long white spaces,
   Where dim leaves are whirling now,
How I gazed on phantom-faces,
   How I planned—no matter how!
Here I wandered, here I pondered,
   Here I made a vow.

Cold crisp renovating weather,
   Clear and colourless and bright,
This, I think, should go together
   With a mind intent on right,
Plans revolving, deeds resolving,
   Seeking for the light.

Yes, I made a vow, and wrote it
   In my heart, nine months ago:
Framed a contract—I could quote it:
   Drew a line to walk by—so:
Have I kept it? or o'erleapt it?
   Well, I hardly know.

Ballade of the Drowning Fusee

The pipe I intend to consume
   Is full, and fairly alight:
It scatters a fragrant perfume,
   Blue smoke-wreaths are heaving in sight:
   I sink on the heathery height,
And lo! there is borne unto me
   From a sweet little stream on my right
The song of the drowning fusee.

The monarch of waterfowl, whom
   On the brink of an infinite night
A strange irresistible doom
   Converts to a musical wight,
   Is akin, in his glory's despite,
To a moribund match, as we see,
   While we listen, in speechless delight,
To the song of the drowning fusee.

As he sinks in his watery tomb,
   His epitaph let me indite.
He hardly took up any room;
   His life was retired; his end bright.
   With destiny no one can fight
All poets and prosers agree,
   And a tribute to destiny's might
Is the song of the drowning fusee.

Friend! would you be gratified quite
   The first of our poets to be?
If so, I advise you to write
   The song of the drowning fusee.

Battle

How seldom it happens in these dull days,
   When we're all decorous, and all behave,
That our pulses can beat at fever heat
   And our deeds be sudden and bright and brave,
In the keen delight of a stand-up fight,
   When the wronger falls and the wronged wins bays.

To know you are right and to say so boldly,
   To prove your strength by a downright blow,
To punish and pound your foe till the ground
   Is red with his blood!—but then, you know,
We "make up a visage"—: the worst of this age
   Is just that we bear our wrongs so coldly.

There's a man—for the matter of that there are men—
   I could deal with just as our fathers dealt
With those who defied their manly pride;
   Oh! to feel the wild delight they felt
When face to face with a foe: disgrace
   To inflict, and glory to win: but then

We've the honour of being so civilised,
   So good, so kind and so truly wise,
And we seldom say at the present day
   "Come on you—" what you can all surmise:—
If we did, we should gain! but it's all in vain,
   And my villains will die unpulverised!

But if I could have what some have prayed for,
    One life more to live how and when I chose,
I would ask to belong to one age when wrong
    Is punished by honest unflinching blows,
When to hate's to fight in the open light,
    And a dire offence is as direly paid for.

Blue Hills. An Allegory

Years ago, in the land of my birth,
When my head was little above the earth,
I stood by the side of the grass-blades tall,
And a quickset hedge was a mighty wall,
And a measureless forest I often found
In a swampy acre of rush-clad ground:
But, when I could see it, the best of the view
Was a distant circle, the Hills of Blue.

Higher we grow as the long years pass,
And I now look down on the growing grass;
I see the top where I saw the side,
Some beauties are lost as the view grows wide,
I see over things that I couldn't see through:
But my limit is still the Hills of Blue.

As a child I sought them, and found them not,
Footsore and weary, tired and hot;
They were still the bulwark of all I could see,
And still at a fabulous distance from me;
I wondered if age and strength could teach
How to traverse the plain, the mountains reach;
Meanwhile, whatever a child might do,
They still were far and they still were blue.

Well I've reached them at last, those distant Hills;
I've reached their base through a world of ills;
I have toiled and laboured and wandered far,
With my constant eyes on a shifting star:
And ever, as nearer I came, they grew,
Larger and larger, but, ah! less blue.

Green I have found them, green and brown,
Studded with houses, o'erhanging a town,
Feeding the plain below with streams,
Dappled with shadows and brightening with beams,
Image of scenes I had left behind,
Merely a group of the hilly kind:
And beyond them a prospect as fair to view
As the old, and bounded by Hills as blue.

But I will not seek those further Hills,
Nor travel the course of the outward rills;
I have lost the faith of my childhood's day;
Let me dream (it is only a dream) while I may;
I will put my belief to no cruel test:
As I doze on this green deceptive crest,
I will try to believe, as I used to do,
There are some Blue Hills which are really blue.

Boating Song. K.B.C.*

Lent 1880 (Air: *It's a fine hunting day*)

On a damp windy day
In tempestuous May,
In a most insufficient attire,
What a pleasure to row
For a furlong or so,
And to glow with a patriot's fire:
There is glory to win in the fray,
There are crowds to applaud all the way,
We shall very soon be
At the top of the tree
If we all go out every day.

Chorus
Let's all go out every day
From now till the middle of May:
We shall very soon be
At the top of the tree
If we all go out every day.

*King's Boat Club

By the top of the tree,
As I think you must see,
It's the head of the river I mean:
An appropriate place
For our vessel to grace
And at which she will shortly be seen:
There are still a few boats in the way,
But Rome is not built in a day,
And I have not a doubt
We shall bring it about
If we all go out every day.

Chorus

Says our captain, says he:—
"May you all of you be
Dissected and roasted and skinned:
Five rowed with his back
In the shape of a sack
And then, when I swore at him, grinned:
Six, get those hands sharper away!
Keep your eyes in the boat there, I say!
Now get on to it, do!
Get that body down, two!
Your time's worse than ever to-day."

Chorus

Both our Tutors are there,
Neither pleasure nor care
Can keep them away from the scene:
And who shouteth so loud
In that jubilant crowd
As each blown but uproarious Dean?
The Provost brings down Mrs A.,
Who runs a good part of the way;
Oscar Browning himself
Throws his gown on the shelf
And dismisses his staff for the day.

Chorus

Cigarettes

I.
I cannot blow rings
    When I am smoking;
I can do many things,
I *cannot* blow rings—
It's a failure that stings,
    For it *is* so provoking;
I cannot blow rings
    When I am smoking.

II.
Life's a cigar,
    And Love is the taper;
Lit at Love's star,
Life's a cigar:
A puff—and we are
    Ashes and vapour.
Life's a cigar,
    And Love is the taper.

Circuit Songs

(Air: Barbara Allen)

1.
In Pembrokeshire where I was born
  Were many maidens dwelling,
But all of them were quite forlorn
  For love of Thomas Allen.

All in the merry month of May,
  When green buds they were swelling,
Some twenty-six on their death-beds lay,
  For love of Thomas Allen.

Then slowly slowly Tom rode round,
  And one by one did eye 'em;
But all that Tom could find to say
  Was:— These poor girls are dying.

And so in course of time they died,
  And all of them were buried,
Excepting one, and she survived,
  And that one Thomas married.

(Air: *Drink to me only*)

2.

Drink to me only with thine eyes and I'll pledge
  thee with mine,
Leave but some coffee in thy cup and I'll not ask
  for wine.
A circuit dinner, as I know, doth ask a drink divine,
Yet would I scorn the mess champagne, could I get
  but that liquor of thine.
I sent thee late a prosy brief, not so much honouring
  thee,
As in the hope that thou wouldst work and I should
  get the fee.
Thou sent'st it back : it was endorsed with judgement
  against me.
'Tis still unpaid and smells I swear of lemonade
  and tea.

Cynicus to W. Shakspere

You wrote a line too much, my sage,
   Of seers the first, and first of sayers;
For only half the world's a stage,
   And only all the women players.

Drinking Song

There are people, I know, to be found,
    Who say and apparently think
That sorrow and care may be drowned
    By a timely consumption of drink.

Does not man, these enthusiasts ask,
    Most nearly approach the divine
When engaged in the soul-stirring task
    Of filling his body with wine?

Have not beggars been frequently known
    When satisfied, soaked and replete,
To imagine their bench was a throne
    And the civilised world at their feet?

Lord Byron has finely described
    The remarkably soothing effect
Of liquor, profusely imbibed,
    On a soul that is shattered and wrecked.

In short, if your body or mind
    Or your soul or your purse come to grief,
You need only get drunk, and you'll find
    Complete and immediate relief.

For myself, I have managed to do
    Without having recourse to this plan,
So I can't write a poem for you,
    And you'd better get someone who can.

Early School

If there is a vile, pernicious,
    Wicked and degraded rule,
Tending to debase the vicious,
    And corrupt the harmless fool;
If there is a hateful habit
    Making man a senseless tool,
With the feelings of a rabbit,
    And the wisdom of a mule:
It's the rule which inculcates,
It's the habit which dictates,
The wrong and sinful practice of going into school.

If there's anything improving
    To an erring sinner's state,
Which is useful in removing
    All the ills of human fate:
If there's any glorious custom
    Which our faults can dissipate,
And can casually thrust 'em
    Out of sight, and make us great:
It's the plan by which we shirk
Half our matutinal work,
The glorious institution of always being late.

Elegy on de Marsay

Come cats and kittens everywhere,
    Whate'er of cat the world contains,
From Tabby on the kitchen stair
To Tiger burning in his lair
    Unite your melancholy strains;

Weep, likewise, kindred dogs, and weep
    Domestic fowls, and pigs, and goats;
Weep horses, oxen, poultry, sheep,
Weep finny monsters of the deep,
    Weep foxes, weasels, badgers, stoats.

Weep more than all, exalted man
    And hardly less exalted maid;
Out-weep creation if you can
Which never yet, since time began,
    Such creditable grief displayed.

It little profiteth that we
    Go proudly up and down the land,
And drive our ships across the sea,
And babble of Eternity,
    And hold the Universe in hand;

If, when our pride is at its height,
    And glory sits upon our head,
A sudden mist can dim the light,
A voice be heard in pride's despite,
    A voice which cries "de Marsay's dead."

De Marsay dead! and never more
   Shall I behold that silky form
Lie curled upon the conscious floor
With sinuous limbs and placid snore,
   As one who sleeps through calm and storm?

De Marsay dead! De Marsay dead!
   And are you dead, de Marsay, you?
The sun is shining over head
With glory undiminishèd,
   And you are dead; let me die too!

Then birds, and beasts, and fishes come,
   And people come, of all degrees;
Beat, sadly beat the funeral drum,
And let the gloomy organ hum
   With dark mysterious melodies.

And (when we've adequately moaned),
   For all the world to wonder at,
Let this great sentence be intoned:
No cat so sweet a mistress owned;
   No mistress owned so sweet a cat.

"Facilis Descensus Averni"

When I was new and all unspoiled,
　　O how I loved examinations!
With what unflagging zeal I toiled!
With what incessant labour soiled
My books! how high my spirit boiled!
　　Till—notwithstanding regulations—
At times the surreptitious oil 'd
　　Assist my midnight lucubrations:
And how my very soul recoiled
At any thought of being foiled
　　By other people's machinations.

Thus, thus the unsuspecting youth
　　Sets forth upon the task of life,
His zeal for seeking abstract truth
　　Is sharpened by his love of strife;
High rise his hopes—his earliest half
Gleig's Wellington in yellow calf,
And Creasy's Battles, side by side,
Excite his own, his parents' pride.
　　But hopes are vain, pride hollow:
The sequel of my tale abide,
　　And mark what needs must follow.

So hard on one another's heels
    The blithe examinations troop,
That soon the young enthusiast feels
    Like flowers do that droop, and droop—
And then a tempest of despair
Sweeps over him: his only care
Is now to find some brilliant, rare,
    And quite unprecedented blunders,
To clear the dull scholastic air,
    And startle Academic thunders.

Then comes the melancholy, vain,
And hopeless struggle to regain
    His old unsullied reputation:
Abortive efforts to attain
    Impossible regeneration:
And, when the last collapse is plain,
No earthly solace doth remain,
    Except to launch an imprecation
That only is not quite profane
Against the author of his pain,
Who brings all evils in his train,
The friend of sloth, ambition's bane,
    The master fiend, Examination.

For Anapaests

Rushing and roaring,
  Dashing around,
Scattering, soaring,
  Icy, profound;
High as the hill-top,
  Glassy and glorious,
Skyey, mellifluous,
  Glad and victorious!

For Greek Iambics

after William Shakespeare

Pe.   Not so, my liege, for even now the town
        Splits with sedition, and the incensed mob
        Rush hither roaring.
Olc.   Let them roar their fill,
        Bluster and bellow till the enormous wings
        Of gusty Boreas flap with less ado.
        Ask they my treacherous nephew's wretched life,
        As if that order were a thing of nought
        Which I did publish? Let them beg or threaten,
        I'll not regard them. Oh my trusty friend,
        There is no rock defies the elements,
        With half the constancy that kinglike men
        Shut up their breasts against such routs as these.
Pe.   O my most valiant lord, I feel 'tis so,
        Permit me to advance against the foe.

(*Olcis and Terranea*, Act IV., Sc. iii.)

God Save Ireland!

(Air: *Tramp, Tramp, Tramp*)

On the fatal gallows tree
Stood the bloody-minded three
   Who had done to death the inoffensive Brett:
But the fact that they were hung
Is as worthy to be sung
   As their wickedness is worthy to forget.

Chorus

God save Ireland from the Land League!
God save Ireland from Parnell!
   Whether on the gallows high
   Or the battle-field they die,
What matter? they are sure to—come to grief.

Men have figured in the dock,
And behind the prison lock,
   Who were fitter for the gallows than the cell:
But the hardest thing they've seen
Is the try-your-weight machine
   Or a prison suit which doesn't fit them well.

Chorus

They disgrace their country's name,
And they know no touch of shame;
    They promote the crimes they never dared have
      done;
But failure and disgrace
Now stare them in the face,
    Their discreditable course is nearly run.

Chorus

Holy William's Prayer.

after Robert Burns

Great power wham Huxley half denied,
Then snirtled at me when I tried,
Wi' lear fu' deep and readin' wide;
    An' intellec';
Wha weel wi' inspiration vied;
    My jinks sae gleck.

Wha gifted me wi' eloquence,
Frammit frae honesty or sense;
Red-wud for wild experiments
    In cuttin' down
Trees, kirks, peace, Union, parties, rents,
    For my renown.

I threap, an' England kens it too,
That gratitude and praise are due,
For makin' me the only true
    An' needfu' licht,
Exalted into public view
    To guide men richt.

I micht be still—I've tried them a'
Tory, Whig, Peelite, Libera';
But felt from each a solemn ca',
    An' I obeyed;
When fu' kenspeckle was their fa'
    For whilk I prayed.

Not mine the fyke if dislocation,
Fruit of wild talk and confiscation,
Jundie this forjeskit nation,
   To mickle skaith.
I'm but the germ disintegration;
    Its life, its breath.

Aiblins that limmer Unity
Maks clishmaclavers o'er me;
But, Lord, ye ken how pure I be;
   Besides, she raves,
Like thae wha trace my property
    To paid for slaves.

I own I've been a haveril,
Anent Green Kirtle; whae's the ill?
Twice, by my talk, I've had my will;
   An' if preserved,
I'll ettle wi' my Home Rule Bill,
    Again a third.

Healy an' Vernon Harcourt bless,
Tanner, Ford, Egan, Morley—yes;
An' *Daily News*, an' Lan' League Pres
   An' all wha've tried,
Frae hate or folly, to depress
    Proud England's pride.

But help me pour envenomed spite
On Goschen, Chamberlain, an' Bright,
An' Hartington—wha thocht they micht
    Just take a sklent.
The blellums canna see things richt,
    Rule gangs like rent.

Wow, but I'll mak' the voters braindge;
My smytrie a' the kingdom range
Wi' mixtie-maxtie caintrips strange;
    An' most ha' made
It gleg and tawie for the change
    Palmerston spaed.

My jawbone many an ane has sped;
My torches mak' a lowin reid;
Noo help me ding the lion deid,
    An' as I fa'
Pu' down the pillars on my heid,
    An' fair smash a'.

I ken in this my supplication
I've shown conspicuous moderation,
An' only fleech that agitation,
    An' sin, and crime,
May shape all Irish legislation
  As they hae mine.

The seeds I sowed, wi' acclamation,
Of transfer without compensation,
Greed, hate, and State tergiversation,
    Will ripe—and then
The crop be gathered by the nation.
    Amen.   Amen.

In Memoriam

1. J. R. Lowell

Lowell: the labours of your noble life,
Your state-craft, and your high poetic skill
Were aye a force that made for union, till
The peace now reigning hushed the ancient strife
Between the mighty land that gave you life,
And that whose kinship distance could not kill.
I think your death has drawn us nearer still!
Now with your praise our island home is rife,
While rings your continent with equal praise;
And here, as there, we sadly quote your lays.
And Lowell! I who knew you, also know
Some that you loved in England, who to-day
Not only share your countless readers' woe,
But mourn a dear old friend that's passed away.

2. The Rt. Hon. H. C. Raikes

No need upon your honoured tomb
    The words *de Mortuis* to write:
For while we mourn your early doom,
    Your merits strike on all men's sight.

The qualities you chanced to want,
    How unimportant they appear:
Whatever fortune did not grant,
    The greatest gift of all was there.

You never deigned by any shift
    Your share of daily toil to shirk:
You had the grand essential gift—
    Capacity for honest work.

By work you lived, by work you died,
    And earned a name, if any can,
That's almost always misapplied,
    An honest English *Working Man*.

And I, who dared in boyhood's day
    To write, in later years to print,
A somewhat disrespectful lay,
    —Though there was naught of malice in't—

Should like to say I'm not the last
   To recognise your sterling worth:
Forgive my strictures of the past,
   The overflow of harmless mirth;

For this at least is wholly true;
   I should be more than satisfied
To work as well and hard as you,
   To die in harness, as you died.

In the Backs

As I was strolling lonely in the Backs,
I met a woman whom I did not like.
I did not like the way the woman walked:
Loose-hipped, big-boned, disjointed, angular.
If her anatomy comprised a waist,
I did not notice it: she had a face
With eyes and lips adjusted thereunto,
But round her mouth no pleasing shadows stirred,
Nor did her eyes invite a second glance.
Her dress was absolutely colourless,
Devoid of taste or shape or character;
Her boots were rather old, and rather large,
And rather shabby, not precisely matched.
Her hair was very far from beautiful
And not abundant: she had such a hat
As neither merits nor expects remark.
She was not clever, I am very sure,
Nor witty nor amusing: well-informed
She may have been, and kind, perhaps, of heart;
But gossip was writ plain upon her face.
And so she stalked her dull unthinking way;
Or, if she thought of anything, it was
That such a one had got a second class,
Or Mrs So-and-So a second child.
I do not want to see that girl again:
I did not like her: and I should not mind
If she were done away with, killed, or ploughed.
She did not seem to serve a useful end:
And certainly she was not beautiful.

4th July, 1882, Malines. Midnight

Belgian, with cumbrous tread and iron boots,
Who in the murky middle of the night,
Designing to renew the foul pursuits
In which thy life is passed, ill-favoured wight,
And wishing on the platform to alight
Where thou couldst mingle with thy fellow brutes,
Didst walk the carriage floor (a leprous sight),
As o'er the sky some baleful meteor shoots:
Upon my slippered foot thou didst descend,
Didst rouse me from my slumbers mad with pain,
And laughedst loud for several minutes' space.
Oh may'st thou suffer tortures without end:
May fiends with glowing pincers rend thy brain,
And beetles batten on thy blackened face!

June 19, 1891

All in a peaceful garden fair,
   One night in leafy June,
There sat a wondrous lovely pair,
   And waited for the Moon,

In silence, save where rustled by
   A little creeping breeze,
Which swept the cobwebs from the sky,
   And scarcely stirred the trees.

The one displayed in form and face
   To ail and sundry comers
The sweet accumulated grace
   Of twenty happy summers.

The other, matronly and calm,
   Was most divinely fair,
And each was stately as a palm,
   And each had pale gold hair.

Between them, where a leafy bough
   Obscured the moonlight pale,
Lounged a vast form with classic brow,
   Unquestionably male.

There rose a mighty yellow Moon,
    Across the tree-tops peering
Along the fleecy sky of June,
    Through which she'll soon be steering.

And when she saw each lovely maid
    She clapped her silver hands;
"Such wondrous charms are rare" she said
    "In all sublunar lands.

"But which is fairest?" long and loud
    She shouted to the stars,
Which glittered in a golden crowd,
    Like newly lit cigars.

Then from the zenith *Vega* slid,
    And red *Aldebaran*
Rushed up the sky, as he was bid,
    To meet the stately *Swan*;

And many dozen more appeared,
    Till all the sky was bare,
And round the Satellite careered,
    And vowed the scene was fair.

Then spake the Moon: "I'm sore distressed:
    "Two beauteous forms I see:
"I can't say which I like the best:
    "Decide the point for me.

"Such foolish puzzles, I declare,
    "I hold in much abhorrence:
"Say if the lovelier of the pair
    "Be A——————— or F———————."

Then peeping o'er each other's head,
    The striking scene to scan,
The Stars unanimously said:—
    "We much prefer the Man."

Köln, 5 July, 1882. 6.30 a.m.

Fair morning sun! bright monarch of the East!
    Thou joy and solace of the human heart,
Who comfortest the greatest and the least,—
    How wonderful, how very fair thou art!

Fair to the horny-handed sons of toil
    Who if they mean to have their daily bread,
Must ply their trade or plough the unyielding soil
    When greasy citizens are still abed.

Fair to the Bard, who oft at early dawn
    Observes the op'ning flow'rs and soaring larks,
And naturally seeks an upland lawn
    Whereon to make poetical remarks.

Fairest to toil-worn travellers who see
    The hard-earned bed display its varied charms:
"Breakfast at 12!" they cry: and seek with glee
    A long repose in Morpheus' downy arms.

Labenti Calamo

Adieu, dear pen! thy merry quips
   And facile cranks have had their day;
Thy not unprofitable "slips"
   Have passed in printer's ink away.

Nor less thy days of serious verse
   On love, and art, and such high themes
Have suffered the primeval curse,
   And died into the realm of dreams.

We are but frauds, the pair of us:
   And if a while you've masqueraded
As quill from wing of Pegasus,
   That little fancy's gone and faded.

You're dying, pen: but I am not:
   You're old; I'm barely middle-aged;
And, while you comfortably rot,
   I shall be otherwise engaged.

I've done my best at stringing rhymes,
   And found it pleasant, goodness knows;
I've shunned some errors, spared some crimes,
   And now I'm going back to prose.

Yes, prose is what I wrote at first,
   And prose is what I'll live by writing,
It's not by any means the worst
   Of trades, nor yet the least exciting.

For, mark you, writing is an art,
   As all but daily hacks acknowledge;
It ought to form the highest part
   Of men's curriculum at College.

It's easy when you've got to scan,
   And got to rhyme before you print,
To make a stanza, where a man
   Shall see of art at least a hint.

But when you're writing prose as pure
   As Jourdain talked, but didn't know it,
You'll have to make, you may be sure,
   Some efforts easier for a poet.

A sentence, lacking rhyme and measure,
   But none the less a work of art,
Costs greater pains, gives greater pleasure
   Than much that's dearer in the mart.

Your half unfinished statuette,
   Or humble tune which 'scapes e'en stealing,
A sketch you make and then forget,
   Has more of art, and more of feeling.

Than some correct colossal bust,
   Or operatic morceau fine,
Which wins encomiums loud and just,
   Or picture hanging on the line.

So such a humble work in prose,
    Which says what has been said before,
Or article, or letter shows,
    To those who know their business, more

Of true artistic worth, my pen,
    Than poetry that's capped and quoted,
Wherever cultivated men
    Praise that to which they're all devoted.

I mean to reappear as one
    Whose prose is better than his verse:
Farewell, my friend through days of fun!
    Farewell, deft liner of my purse!

We've lived right gaily you and I:
    We've had some sport, and made some money:
And, if we could not make folks cry.
    We *were* occasionally funny.

We've argued too in verse: we've tried
    To prove, disprove, deny, assert;
We've blustered, whispered, laughed and sighed,
    But never yet did any hurt.

Yet both were certain all the time,
    As any candid friend could be,
That though we might succeed in rhyme
    We could not rise to poetry.

The curtain falls: the play is done:
    But I am in another piece:
I've got to dress: the band's begun
    It's time for our discourse to cease.

I go to fly at higher game:
    At prose as good as I can make it:
And, though it brings nor gold nor fame,
    I will not, while I live, forsake it.

Farewell! I've other work to do:
    Another way of reaching men:
But I shall still remember you
    You've served me well: adieu, dear Pen!

Lapsus Calami

I played with pen and ink at times,
    Until upon my table grew
A little heap of random rhymes:
    I got them printed, bound in blue,
And sold for more than they were worth,
To cause a moment's harmless mirth.

My little book achieved success,
    And wandered up and down the land;
A thousand copies more or less
    Were sold and paid for; that was grand;
And I was honestly surprised
To be so kindly criticised.

And when the little book was sold,
    I threw away the half of it;
And to the remnant of the old
    I tacked some new attempts at wit;
To which I added here and there
Some work prepared with greater care;

Some work in which I tried to shew
    That clowns can reason, jesters feel;
Nor need a scribbler lack the glow
    Of passion, or the fire of zeal
Because his verse is fairly neat,
And tries, at least, to be complete.

And having managed to acquire
    A public (as a fool I speak),
I thought to aim a little higher,
    A more substantial prize to seek;
And now I mean to write a book
Where men for fewer jests must look.

Kind readers who have borne with me
    When I confessed my school-boy rhymes,
And bought what purported to be
    A jest-book, turning grave at times,
I scarcely dare to hope that still
You'll read me: but perhaps you will.

And if you should insert me—Yes,
    You know the rest? upon the list
Of lyric bards—I ask no less—
    My head, if not precisely kissed
By stars, will wear at least a crown
Preferred to that which decks the clown.

Lines at the River Side

Showing how the Poet was unfortunately disappointed of a most Tragic Theme

'Tis but a work of the loom,
   'Tis but a shawl on the grass,
   'Tis but a remnant, alas!
Remnant of what and of whom?

Surely some victim of woe
   Left it to bleach on the brink,
   Left it to plunge and to sink
Under the waters below.

Doubt, hesitation and fear,
   Madness, delusion, despair,
   All of them culminate there,
There by the swift rushing weir.

Was it a husband she fled,
   Drunken, of reason bereft?
   Was it a child that she left
Peaceful and pale in its bed?

Rash was the folly, I trow,
   Vice got the best of the strife.
   One little moment of life!
What would she give for it now?

Ha! what has shattered it all?
  How is my muse disarray'd?
  Only a nursery maid
Come back to look for her shawl.

Lines written at "Private"

It's very dull no doubt
    Hearing Whalley prate,
Dull to hear Kenealy spout
    When he grows irate,
Dull to be harangued about
    Nuns by Newdegate.
Very dull is all of this,
    Very dull and dry,
But it is surpassed, I wis,
    Most completely by
"Caii Julii Caesaris
    Commentarii."

Midsummer

after Robert Browning

Persons at various times have said
   That the hot dank steam of a sun-scorched day
Is a thing to thank God for: strike me dead
   If I let such a falsehood lack its nay.

When Philip of Spain, or our own red Mary,
   Desired to be rid of an impious man,
Did they *freeze* him to death? they were not so chary
   Of man's worst weapon, the frying pan.

The fire, or the frying pan—well, the adage
   Tells us the difference is but small,
And the fact remains that in that last bad age
   When man had all torture-tricks at call,

They knew what was best and did it duly,
   And broiled those most whom they loved the least.
Man, is it thou that hast proved unruly?
   They are broiling thee, thou sinful beast.

Languid and frenzied, most despairing
   When least's to despair at, such we grow,
When the sun's rays down on our heads, naught
     sparing,
   Burn and blister.   I'd have you know

I have strung together these sad reflections
   To prove to my tutor, a stern stark man,
That my chance of a decent place in collections
   Drooped and died when the heat began.

My Education

At school I sometimes read a book,
    And learned a lot of lessons;
Some small amount of pains I took,
    And showed much acquiescence
In what my masters said, good men!
    Yet after all I quite
Forgot the most of it: but then
                        I learned to write.

At Lincoln's Inn I'd read a brief,
    Abstract a title, study
Great paper-piles, beyond belief
    Inelegant and muddy:
The whole of these as time went by
    I soon forgot: indeed
I tried to: yes: but by and by
                        I learned to read.

By help of Latin, Greek and Law
    I now can write and read too:
Then perish each forgotten saw,
    Each fact I do not need too:
But still whichever way I turn
    At one sad task I stick:
I fear that I shall never learn
                        Arithmetic.

My Old School

There's a long low wall with trees behind it,
    And an old grey chapel behind the trees,
Neath the shade of a royal keep you'll find it,
    Where Kings and Emperors take their ease.

There's another wall, with a field beside it,
    A wall not wholly unknown to fame;
For a game's played there which most who've tried it
    Declare is a truly noble game.

There's a great grey river that swirls and eddies
    To the Bells of Ouseley from Boveney Weir,
With willowy stumps where the river's bed is,
    And rippling shallows, and spaces clear.

There's a cloistered garden and four quadrangles,
    And red brick buildings both old and new:
There's a bell that tolls, and a clock that jangles,
    And a stretch of sky that is often blue.

There's a street that's alive with boys and masters:
    And ah! there's a feeling of home for me:
For my boyhood's triumphs, delights, disasters,
    Successes and failures were here, you see.

And if sometimes I've laughed in my rhymes at Eton,
    Whose glory I never could jeopardise,
Yet I'd never a joy that I could not sweeten,
    Or a sorrow I could not exorcise,

By the thought of my school, and the brood that's
    bred there,
  Her bright boy faces, and keen young life:
And the manly stress of the hours that sped there,
  And the stirring pulse of her daily strife.

For, mark, when an old friend meets another
  Who have lived and remembered for years apart,
And each is as true as to best-loved brother,
  And each has a faithful and tender heart;

Do they straight spread arms, and profess devotion,
  And exhibit the signs of a heartfelt joy?
No; but each stands steady, and scorns emotion,
  And each says:—How do you do, old boy?

And so, old school, if I lightly greet you,
  And have laughed at your foibles these fifteen
    years,
It is just as a dear old friend I treat you,
  And the smile on my lips is a mask for tears:

And it is not a form of words, believe me,
  To say I am yours while my pulses beat,
And whatever garlands the fates may weave me
  I'll lay right gladly at Eton's feet.

Ode on a retrospect of Eton College

after Thomas Gray

Ye bigot spires, ye Tory towers,
    That crown the watery lea,
Where grateful science still adores
    The aristocracy:
A happy usher once I strayed
Beneath your lofty elm trees' shade,
    With mind untouched by guilt or woe:
But mad ambition made me stray
Beyond the round of work and play
    Wherein we ought to go.

My office was to teach the young
    Idea how to shoot:
But, ah! I joined with eager tongue
    Political dispute:
I ventured humbly to suggest
That all things were not for the best
    Among the Irish peasantry:
And finding all the world abuse
My simple unpretending views,
    I thought I'd go and see.

I boldly left the College bounds:
    Across the sea I went,

To probe the economic grounds
   Of Irish discontent.
My constant goings to and fro
Excited some alarm; and so
   Policemen girded up their loins,
And, from his innocent pursuits,—
Morose unsympathetic brutes,—
   They snatched a fearful Joynes.

Escaped, I speedily returned
   To teach the boys again:
But ah, my spirit inly burned
   To think on Ireland's pain.
Such wrongs must out: and then, you see,
My own adventures might not be
   Uninteresting to my friends:
I therefore ventured to prepare
A little book, designed with care,
   To serve these humble ends.

Our stern head-master spoke to me
   Severely:—"You appear
"(*Horresco referens*) to be
   "A party pamphleteer.
"If you *must* write, let Caesar's page
"Or Virgil's poetry engage
   "Your all too numerous leisure hours:
"But now annihilate and quash
"This impious philanthropic bosh:
   "Or quit these antique towers."

It seems that he who dares to write
  Is all unfit to teach:
And literary fame is quite
  Beyond an usher's reach.
I dared imprisonment in vain:
The little bantling of my brain
  I am compelled to sacrifice.
The moral, after all, is this:—
That here, where ignorance is bliss,
  'Tis folly to be wise.

Ode on the 450th Anniversary Celebration at Eton

Think of a number: double it
(If that does not surpass thy wit);
Subtract a dozen: add a score:
Divide by twenty: multiply
By twice the cube of $x + y$,
And half again as many more:
Then take the twenty-seventh root
And logarithmic sine to boot,
And if the answer does not show
Just nine times fifty, make it so.

There's something more than half divine
In fifty multiplied by nine:
And never integer has been
So grand as thirty times fifteen:
The total I could doubtless praise
In many other striking ways:
But this at least is very plain,—
The same will never come again.

Then make an exhibition please
And summon guests from far and wide:
And marry mystic melodies
To odes instinct with proper pride.
Invoke the Founder's mighty name,
And boast of Gray's and Shelley's fame:
For this is very sure: that we
Who missed the latest jubilee
Shall not improbably be vexed
By missing equally the next.

Then let us resolutely strive
This mighty fact to keep alive
That 5 times 9 is 45;
    And furthermore the truth to fix
(In their behoof whose course will run
In June of 1981)
    That 54 is 9 times 6.

On a Parisian Boulevard

Britannia rules the waves,
    As I have heard her say;
She frees whatever slaves
    She meets upon her way.

A teeming mother she
    Of Parliaments and Laws;
Majestic, mighty, free:
    Devoid of common flaws.

For her did Shakspere write
    His admirable plays:
For her did Nelson fight
    And Wolseley win his bays.

Her sturdy common sense
    Is based on solid grounds:
By saving numerous pence
    She spends effective pounds.

The Saxon and the Celt
    She equitably rules;
Her iron rod is felt
    By countless knaves and fools.

In fact, mankind at large,
    Black, yellow, white and red,
Is given to her in charge,
    And owns her as a head.

But every here and there—
    Deny it if you can—
She breeds a vacant stare
    Unworthy of a man:

A look of dull surprise;
    A nerveless idle hand:
An eye which never tries
    To threaten or command:

In short, a kind of man,
    If man indeed he be,
As worthy of our ban
    As any that we see:

Unspeakably obtuse,
    Abominably vain,
Of very little use,
    And execrably plain.

On a Rhine Steamer

Republic of the West,
   Enlightened, free, sublime,
Unquestionably best
   Production of our time.

The telephone is thine,
   And thine the Pullman Car,
The caucus, the divine
   Intense electric star.

To thee we likewise owe
   The venerable names
Of Edgar Allan Poe,
   And Mr Henry James.

In short it's due to thee,
   Thou kind of Western star,
That we have come to be
   Precisely what we are.

But every now and then,
   It cannot be denied,
You breed a kind of men
   Who are not dignified,

Or courteous or refined,
   Benevolent or wise,
Or gifted with a mind
   Beyond the common size,

Or notable for tact,
   Agreeable to me,
Or anything, in fact,
   That people ought to be.

On the King's Parade

As I was waiting for the tardy tram,
I met what purported to be a man.
What seemed to pass for its material frame,
The semblance of a suit of clothes had on,
Fit emblem of the grand sartorial art
And worthy of a more sublime abode.
Its coat and waistcoat were of weird design
Adapted to the fashion's latest whim.
I think it wore an Athenæum tie.
White flannels draped its too ethereal limbs
And in its vacant eye there glared a glass.

  In vain for this poor derelict of flesh,
Void of the spirit it was built to house,
Have classic poets tuned their deathless lyre,
Astute historians fingered mouldering sheets
And reared a palace of sententious truth.
In vain has y been added unto x,
In vain the mighty decimal unrolled,
Which strives indefinitely to be π.
In vain the palpitating frog has groaned
Beneath the licensed knife: in vain for this
The surreptitious corpse been disinterred
And forced, amid the disinfectant fumes,
To yield its secrets to philosophy.
In vain the stress and storm of politics

Beat round this empty head: in vain the priest
Pronounces loud anathemas: the fool
In vain remarks upon the fact that God
Is missing in the world of his belief.
Vain are the problems whether space, or time,
Or force, or matter can be said to be:
Vain are the mysteries of Melchisedec,
And vain Methuselah's unusual years.

   It had a landlady I make no doubt;
A friend or two as vacant as itself;
A kitchen-bill; a thousand cigarettes;
A dog which knew it for the fool it was.
Perhaps it was a member of the Union,
Who votes as often as he does not speak,
And "recommends" as wildly as he spells.
Its income was as much beyond its merits
As less than its inane expenditure.
Its conversation stood to common sense
As stands the *Sporting Times* (its favourite print)
To wit or humour. It was seldom drunk,
But seldom sober when it went to bed.

   The mean contents of these superior clothes
Were they but duly trained by careful hands,
And castigated with remorseless zeal,
Endowed with purpose, gifted with a mind,
And taught to work, or play, or talk, or laugh,
Might possibly aspire—I do not know—
To pass, in time, for what they dare to scorn,
An ordinary undergraduate.

What did this thing crawling 'twixt heaven and earth,
Amid the network of our grimy streets?
What end was it intended to subserve,
What lowly mission fashioned to neglect?
It did not seem to wish for a degree,
And what its object was I do not know,
Unless it was to catch the tardy tram.

Paint and Ink

*To C. W. F.**

You take a brush, and I take a pen:
    You mix bright colours, I use black ink:
You cover a canvas, you first of men,
    I write on a sheet for a scribbler meet:
Well, a contrast's a contrast: I will not shrink.

First you compose: a line's grand sweep,
    A break, a blend, a guide for our eyes:
You've a tone to settle, a curve to keep,
    An impression to catch, new tints to match;
And a lesson behind it surely lies.

And every touch of your busy brush,
    And every scrape of your palette-knife,
Each squeeze of the tube whence the pigments gush,
    Each rub of your thumb, helps the whole become
A living page from the scroll of life.

There's a landscape, a face, which displays—you
        know it—
    A fact, a fancy, a thought, a dream,
Which the many miss; so, my picture-poet,
    You catch a part not the whole,—that's art,—
And fix if for ever: a simpler theme

*Charles Wellington Furse

For a man to grasp at, conceive, remember,
    Than that which you saw and which we see not:
There's your *Bathing Girl* and your *Bleak December*,
    Which you paint and exhibit for fools to gibbet:
You wrote the play, but God gave the plot.

And we in the pit have caught the meaning
    You caught, or so much as you saved for us;
But here I perceive you intervening,
    I hear your stricture: "A picture's a picture:
Colour and form:" well! come, discuss.

Is there nothing but colour and form? no soul?
    A judicious blend, an arrangement clever:
Reds and blues: lines curves: and is that the whole?
    No hint designed of the truth behind:
Just a thing of beauty, a joy for ever!

I think you are wronging yourself my friend,
    And the noble craft that you ply so well:
For colour and form have a certain end,
    And composition, or else ambition
Were better bestowed than on paint: you tell

New truths to us; draw for us morals old
    From what seemed to have no moral at all:
And all's not done when your picture's sold,
    Nor when you're R.A., at a future day,
And your picture glows on a palace wall.

To see, and to paint; and to know at sight
   How much wants painting, how much neglect,
Is a noble function, I know: you're right:
   But by nature's laws there is never a cause
That cannot or does not produce effect.

And, to point the contrast, and draw the moral,
   I too, with my humbler art, aspire
To a name which I hope you will not quarrel
   To see me claim: to the noble name
Of an artist: in truth I know no higher.

But the metres I choose, and the rules I keep,
   And the lilt of the verses I write for sport,
And the rhythm of lines that have made you sleep,
   And the style of my prose, which, goodness knows,
Might grow far better and still fall short;

All these, were they better, or even free
   From faults, would never enable you
In the scribbler a brother in arms to see
   In the noble fray which you fight to day
For the good, the beautiful and the true.

I've thoughts to interpret and truths to teach,
   I've an unread lesson at first to read,
Then to state so much of as e'er can reach
   The brain of the man in the street: my plan
Is the same as your own, Sir, it is indeed!

I blend and arrange and compose: subdue
   And indicate, aye and emphasize:
Till the world gets a hint of the truth: and you?
   You do just the same, and the artist's name
Is for writer and painter the highest prize.

Your colour and form, my words and style,
   Your wondrous brush and my busy pen,
Are our medium, our tools: and all the while
   The question for each is what truths we teach
And how we interpret the world to men.

So I do dare claim to be kin with you,
   And I hold you higher than if your task
Were doing no more than you say you do:
   We shall live, if at all, we shall stand or fall,
As men before whom the world doffs its mask
And who answer the questions our fellows ask.

Parker's Piece, *May* 19, 1891

To see good *Tennis*! what diviner joy
Can fill our leisure, or our minds employ?
Not *Sylvia's* self is more supremely fair,
Than balls that hurtle through the conscious air.
Not *Stella's* form instinct with truer grace
Than *Lambert's* racket poised to win the *chase*.
Not *Chloe's* harp more native to the ear,
Than the tense strings which smite the flying sphere.
   When *Lambert boasts* the superhuman *force*,
Or splits the echoing *grille* without remorse:
When *Harradine*, as graceful as of yore,
Wins *better than a yard*, upon the floor;
When *Alfred's* ringing cheer proclaims success,
Or *Saunders volleys* in resistlessness;
When *Heathcote's service* make the *dedans* ring
With just applause, and own its honoured king;
When *Pettitt's* prowess all our zeal awoke
Till high Olympus shuddered at the stroke;
Or, when, receiving *thirty and the floor*,
The novice *serves* a dozen *faults* or more;

Or some plump don, perspiring and profane,
Assails the roof and breaks the exalted pane;
When *vantage, five games all, the door* is called,
And Europe pauses, breathless and appalled,
Till lo! the ball by cunning hand caressed
Finds in the *winning gallery* a nest;
These are the moments, this the bliss supreme,
Which makes the artist's joy, the poet's dream.

    Let *cricketers* await the tardy sun,
Break one another's shins and call it fun;
Let *Scotia's golfers* through the affrighted land
With crooked knee and glaring eye-ball stand;
Let *football* rowdies show their straining thews,
And tell their triumphs to a mud-stained Muse;
Let *india-rubber* pellets dance on *grass*
Where female arts the ruder sex surpass;
Let other people play at other things;
The *king of games* is still the *game of kings*.

Poetic lamentation on the insufficiency of steam locomotion in the Lake district

after William Wordsworth

Bright Summer spreads his various hue
   O'er nestling vales and mountains steep,
Glad birds are singing in the blue,
   In joyous chorus bleat the sheep.
But men are walking to and fro,
   Are riding, driving far and near,
And nobody as yet can go
   By train to Buttermere.

The sunny lake, the mountain track,
   The leafy groves are little gain,
While Rydal's pleasant pathways lack
   The rattle of the passing train.
But oh! what poet would not sing
   That heaven-kissing rocky cone,
On whose steep side the railway king
   Shall set his smoky throne?

Helvellyn in those happy days
   With tunnelled base and grimy peak
Will mark the lamp's approaching rays,
   Will hear the whistle's warning shriek:
Will note the coming of the mails,
   And watch with unremitting stare
The dusky grove of iron rails
   Which leads to Euston-square.

Wake, England, wake! 'tis now the hour
   To sweep away this black disgrace—
The want of locomotive power
   In so enjoyable a place.
Nature has done her part, and why
   Is mightier man in his to fail?
I want to hear the porters cry,
    "Change here for Ennerdale!"

Man! nature must be sought and found
   In lonely pools, on verdant banks;
Go, fight her on her chosen ground,
   Turn shapely Thirlmere into tanks:
Pursue her to her last retreats,
   And if perchance a garden plot
Is found among the London streets,
   Smoke, steam and spare it not.

Presumptuous nature! do not rate
   Unduly high thy humble lot,
Nor vainly strive to emulate
   The fame of Stephenson and Watt.
The beauties which thy lavish pride
   Has scattered through the smiling land
Are little worth till sanctified
   By man's completing hand.

Question and Answer

*To H. R.**

The Question

The river is flowing,
    The stars coming forth:
Great ruddy clouds going
    From Westward to North:

The rushes are waving,
    The water's still blue:
And I am behaving
    Decorously too:

The amorous zephyr
    Breathes soft in our ear:
Who hears not is deafer
    Than adders, my dear:

Ah! list to the whisper
    Of waters and sky!
Thames, vagabond lisper,
    Grows subtle and sly.

How trebly delicious
    The air-draughts we quaff:
The hour is propitious:—
    Oh!... why do you laugh?

*Herbert Ryle

The Answer

Ask the sky why it flushes,
   The clouds why they glow:
The weir why it gushes,
   The reeds why they grow;

The moon why it rises,
   The sun why it sets:
Her why she surprises,
   Him why he forgets;

The star why it twinkles,
   The west why it shines:
The brow why it wrinkles,
   The heart why it pines:

Mankind why they blunder,
   The corn why there's chaff:
Ask yourself why you wonder—
   Not me why I laugh!

Reflections

1.
Seven days complete the weekly round,
   Seven angels scatter plagues in heaven.
The Reflector yearly costs one pound
                    Seven.

It is edited by Mr. Bevan,
   Yet no hoarding holds his picture, gowned
In a twisted towel to wield the levin;
   It contains a roundel to astound
By its merit (marvellously even).
   "In which number may this gem be found?"
                    Seven.

2.
A candid friend who read the first *Reflector*,
   Sent gratis (for he seldom cares to spend,
Subscribes to nothing, and avoids his rector,
               This candid friend),

Prognosticates the paper's speedy end,
   Dislikes its tone, wishes it were selecter,
Its price and politics alike offend.
   But those who take it in, they do not hector,
They read, enjoy it, o'er its pages bend;
   The "slaves who pay" can laugh at this objector,
               A candid friend.

Regrets

You would not hear me speak; you never knew,
    Will never know, the eloquence unique
It was my purpose to bestow on you;
        You would not hear me speak.

Dear! it was no caprice, or idle freak:
    Perhaps I did not even mean to woo:
My meaning was not very far to seek:
    I might have gained the end I had in view;
I might have failed, since words are often weak;
    It never can be settled now: adieu!
        You would not hear me speak.

Senex to Matt. Prior

Ah! Matt.: old age has brought to me
Thy wisdom, less thy certainty:
The world's a jest, and joy's a trinket:
I knew that once: but now—I think it.

Steam-Launches on the Thames

Henley, June 7, 1891

Shall we, to whom the stream by right belongs,
Who travel silent, save, perchance, for songs;
Whose track's a ripple,—leaves the Thames a lake,
Nor frights the swan—scarce makes the rushes shake;
Who harmonize, exemplify, complete
And vivify a scene already sweet:
Who travel careless on, from lock to lock,
Oblivious that the world contains a clock,
With pace commensurate to our desires,
Propelled by other force than Stygian fire's;
Shall we be driven hence to leave a place
For these, who bring upon our stream disgrace:
The rush, the roar, the stench, the smoke, the steam,
The nightmare striking through our heavenly dream;
The scream as shrill and hateful to the ear
As when a peacock vents his rage and fear;
Which churn to fury all a glassy reach,
And heave rude breakers on a pebbly beach:
Which half o'erwhelm with waves our frailer craft,
While graceless shop-boys chuckle fore and aft:
Foul water-toadstools, noisome filth-stained shapes,
Fit only to be manned by dogs and apes:
Blots upon nature: scars that mar her smile:
Obscene, obtrusive, execrable, vile?

Telepathy

after Frederic W. H. Myers

To A. T. M. *

Good Mr. K., in sturdy self-reliance,
   Thoughtful and placid as a brooding dove,
Stands firmly sucking, in the cause of science,
   Just such a peppermint as schoolboys love.

Suck, placid K.! The world will be thy debtor;
   Though thy mouth water, and thy heart grow faint,
Suck, and the less thou likest it the better;
   Such for our sake and utter no complaint.

See'st thou yon Being, passionate and gentle,
   Man's latest teacher, wisdom's pioneer,
Calmly, majestically monumental?
   X., the august Telepathist, is here.

Waves of perception, subtle emanations,
   Thrill through the ether, circulate amain;
Delicate, soft, impalpable sensations
   Born of thy palate, quiver in his brain.

*Arthur Thomas Marson

Lo! with a voice unspeakably dramatic,
    Lo! with a gesture singularly fine,
He makes at last a lucid and emphatic
    Statement of what is in that mouth of thine.

He could detect that peppermint's existence,
    He read its nature in the book of doom,
Standing at some considerable distance,
    Standing, in fact, in quite another room.

Was there a faint impenetrable essence
    Wafted towards him from the sucking K.?
Did some thin ghost inform him of its presence?
    Or did it happen in some other way?

These are the questions nobody can answer,
    These are the problems nobody can solve;
Only we know that Man is an Advancer;
    Only we know the centuries revolve.

The Ballade of the Incompetent Ballade-Monger

I am not ambitious at all:
   I am not a poet, I know
(Though I do love to see a mere scrawl
   To order and symmetry grow).
   My muse is uncertain and slow,
I am not expert with my tools,
   I lack the poetic *argot:*
But I hope I have kept to the rules.

When your brain is undoubtedly small,
   'Tis hard, sir, to write in a row,
Some five or six rhymes to Nepaul,
   And more than a dozen to Joe:
   The metre is easier though,
Three rhymes are sufficient for 'ghouls,'
   My lines are deficient in go,
But I hope I have kept to the rules.

Unable to fly let me crawl,
   Your patronage kindly bestow:
I am not the author of Saul,
   I am not Voltaire or Rousseau:
   I am not desirous, oh no!
To rise from the ranks of the fools,
   To shine with Gosse, Dobson and Co.:
But I hope I have kept to the rules.

Dear Sir, though my language is low,
   Let me dip in Pierian pools:
My verses are only so so,
   But I hope I have kept to the rules.

The Critic's Speech

"Just the book to review!" the critic cried,
    The Chase of the Snark to wit,
While his audience pressed round him on every side,
    To hear his opinion of it.

"They read it with glasses, they read it with care,
    They peruse it again and again,
They ruin their health beyond repair,
    And they give themselves Snark on the brain.

"But what are the charms of this curious tale,
    Which attract such a numerous band,
Or why it obtains so extensive a sale,
    I could never at all understand.

"The reader who looks through his various books
    Five characteristics will mark,
Which always belong, both in prose and in song,
    To the author of 'Hunting the Snark.'

"The first is the binding: especially that
    Of the book we presume to review,
On which is depicted a watery flat
    Of a sickly cadaverous hue.

"That he's most inconsistent, I think you'll agree,
    When he dares to assert it as true,
That the rudder gets mixed with the bowsprit at sea,
    Or that birds can be salted in glue.

"The third is his manner of making a jest,
　Which is quite and entirely his own,
And he seeks after witty remarks with a zest
　That might find the philosopher's stone.

"The fourth is the way that he sticks to a word,
　Such as beamish, galumph, and the rest,
Which he thinks is amusing as well as absurd,
　An opinion I beg to contest.

"The fifth is pure folly. It now will be just
　To describe each particular vein,
Distinguishing 'fits' which appal and disgust,
　From 'fits' which are simply inane.

"For though much is as pointless as can be desired,
　I'm exceedingly sorry to say
That Kenealy—" the critic abruptly retired,
　For his audience had melted away.

The Dawn of the Year

Once in the year, if you get up early,
    You may get—just once—what you can't but praise:
Not a sky that's blue, or a lawn that's pearly,
    Though these may be there as on other days:
But a bright cool still delicious thrill,
    Which tells you October is come or near:—
                            The Dawn of the Year!

For I take it the end of the Long Vacation
    Which repeoples the Temple and Lincoln's Inn,
And quickens the pulse of civilisation,
    And ends the hush of our daily din,
Is really the season, by light of reason,
    Which ought to and does to the wise appear
                            The Dawn of the Year.

Years die in July and are dead till September:
    By the first of October the New Year's born:
It's a sturdy infant in mid December,
    And reaches its prime some April morn:
Hot and weary in June, it must perish soon,
    It is working too hard: it will break: but *here*
                            Is the Dawn of the Year.

And this is the time for good resolutions:
    He's a laggard who waits till Christmas past:
In obedience to meaningless institutions

He starts on a year which can but last
Six months or so: while we, who know,
   Find in golden autumn, not winter drear,
                        The Dawn of the Year.

You surely remember the feeling I mean?
   It's a misty morning, portending heat:
Scarce a leaf has fallen, the trees are green,
   And the last late flowers are bright and sweet,
By the sight and scent summer's not yet spent,
   But there's something new in the atmosphere.
                        The Dawn of the Year.

Just a touch of healthy autumnal cold,
   Not the dismal shiver of rainy summers;
And a sun no longer a blaze of gold
   To light the frolic of idle mummers,
But a genial guide for the busy tide
   Of men who have work to do, shows clear
                        The Dawn of the Year.

So back to work in the London streets,
   Or College courts, or clamorous Schools;
We have tasted and dwelt on the passing sweets
Of sunlit leisure: resume your tools,
Get back to your labours, my excellent neighbours,
   And greet with a spirit that work can cheer,
                        The Dawn of the Year.

The Fellows' Garden

King's College Cambridge

Sitting on a garden-seat,
  All a summer afternoon,
Reading, while the envious heat
  Haunts you like a weary tune:
Watching other people playing,
  Playing at a certain game;
Bodies flitting, twisting, swaying:
White balls flying, white forms vying
  With each other: can you blame
One who says: "The worst of men is
He who first devised Lawn-Tennis"?

In a villa's garden plot
  Such a game might be allowed:
When a London square grows hot,
  Let a fashionable crowd
Gather, where the brown turf hardens,
  With their Sunday hats and racquets:
But in perfect College gardens
Made for leisure, rife with pleasure,
  Where men go in flannel jackets,
Read their books, and dream their dreams,
Forge their future volumes' themes;

Is it decent, is it right,
   That a man should have to look at
Such a desolating sight,
   One so made to throw a book at,
As a little don that's prancing,
   With a wild, perspiring air,
All about the court is dancing,
Gallopading, masquerading,
   Though nor grace nor strength be there
As an athlete? Let him do it
Somewhere else, or duly rue it.

Nay, more: it was here, was it not,
   That we wandered, two friends and I,
Past the end of June, when a large half-moon
   Sailed sad in a sober sky,
And the trees that were leafy and thick forgot
   To be green, and the mist-wreaths wandered by.

And the world beyond was a dim expanse
   Of blue that was green, and green that was blue,
And the bushes were black which enclosed our track,
   And the flowers were dashed with a blackness too,
And caught in a rapture, or rapt in a trance,
   The garden was waiting: such hours are few!

For at first there were remnants of rosy light
   On the tall grey chapel beyond the trees,
And the west not ablaze, but aglow with rays
   That had faded: a whisper of rest the breeze,
And the silence a tremulous still delight,
   And the unseen meadows as unseen seas.

And we noted a spot where the purple shade,
   Which hid the tree-trunks and dimmed the grass,
Seemed to mean far more than it meant before,
   Till all that we fancied took shape and was:
And we looked on a deep, reposeful glade,
   Whence Satyr and Dryad and Faun might pass.

And that's what the garden must mean for me,
   For me and my friends who were there that night:
What wonder, then, if I hate the men
   Who prove beyond doubt, when the noon is bright,
That my glade is a lawn which can easily be
   Deformed with horrible squares of white,
   And peopled with forms that offend my sight.

The Found Leader

(Air: *Molly Malone*)

'Tis Justin Macarthy
That now leads our party:
   He was born in the beautiful city of Cork:
He has wrote for quare papers,
And cut some quare capers,
   And got through a wonderful deal of loose talk:

He once drove his barrow
Through streets wide and narrow
   Singing novels, bad novels and other bad books:
      And other bad boo-ooks
      And other bad boo-ooks,
   Singing novels, bad novels and other bad books!

He consults pretty freely
With Timothy Healy,
   And is mighty polite to the former Lord Mayor:
And he'll often be sighing
That William O'Brien
   And good Mr Dillon can never be there:

      But he once &c. &c.

The devices of Parnell
Are truly infarnal
    And he fights like a man with his back to the
        wall:
But the divil is in it
If Justin can't win it,
    For bedad he can keep the commandments and all:

    But he once drove &c. &c.

The Gondola

We do not speak, but hearken
  To softly plashing oars,
We watch the wide way darken
  Between the lighted shores,
While sable-hulled and silver-prowed
  Slide past the phantom boats,
And near and far, now low, now loud,
  A drifting music floats;
They only have one song to sing,
The song of youth and love and spring.

And where St. George's Island
  Looms o'er the dark lagoon,
Slow through the rifts of sky-land
  Sails up the golden moon.
Now I can see your shadowy hair
  And read your dreaming eyes,
So sweet, almost the old despair
  The dirge of memory dies;
Oh, only teach me to forget,
And I may learn to love you yet.

The Grand Old Pipe

I have ceased to believe in the Leader
  Whom I loved in the days of my youth:
Is he, or am I the seceder?
  It were hard to determine the truth.
But my enmity is not impassioned:
  I'll forgive and forget if I can,
And I'm smoking a pipe which is fashioned
  Like the face of the Grand Old Man.

It was made in the days when his collars
  Were still of the usual size,
And before the recipients of dollars
  Were known as his trusted allies:
But I love, as I lounge in the garden,
  Or work at my chambers, to gaze
At the face of the master of Hawarden,
  As he was in the Grand Old Days.

My pipe was my one consolation
  When its antitype kindled the flame
Which threatened the brave population
  Of Ulster with ruin and shame:
I forgot that our ruler was dealing
  With scamps of the Sheridan type,
While the true orange colour was stealing
  O'er the face of my Grand Old Pipe.

Did his conduct grow ever absurder
    Till no remnant of reason seemed left?
Did he praise the professors of murder?
    Does he preach the evangel of theft?
When he urges our eloquent neighbours
    To keep other men's land in their gripe,
Grows he black in his face with his labours?
    Well, so does my Grand Old Pipe.

For the sake of its excellent savour,
    For the many sweet smokes of the past,
My pipe keeps it hold on my favour,
    Tho' now it is blackening fast:
And, remembering how long he has striven,
    And the merits he used to possess,
And his fall, let him now be forgiven,
    Though he has made a Grand Old Mess.

The Hundred Yards Race

after Sir Walter Scott

You ask me for a prophecy
About the hundred: I reply
That man can do no more than try;
And so commence and cast about
To find the lucky athletes out.
The goddess of the football field
Some valuable hints may yield:
Inured to grisly war's alarms:
She knows of many a feat of arms,
Full many a tale has she to tell
Of those who nobly fight and well:
'Twas hers to sing the artful J.,
Whose progress nothing could delay:
Twas hers to sing Hunt's reckless rush
Through flooded fields and slimy slush,
The while with gentle words he tried
To win like prowess from his side.
These, and a host of such as they,
She sings no longer, sad to say:
　　But champions still remain
Who furnish many a glorious theme
Until the past doth almost seem
　　To live in them again.

For now the war-like goddess sings,
Obedient to my questionings,
Of Douglas's unrivalled grace,
Of Elliot foremost in the race,
And Stephen's more majestic pace:
Of Chitty's meteoric flight,
And Anderson as swift as light;
Hawke's rapid swoop upon the ball,
Wellesley who never tires at all
   Whate'er of toil betide:
Macaulay's oft repeated bound,
Swift Bayley's feet that shun the ground,
   The Professional stride:
Of Bryan Farrer fast as strong,
Of Lawrence' limbs so lithe and long,
Of Booth's wild gallop in the van,
   She sings the deathless praise:
How stoutly Polhill-Turner ran,
How Spring-Rice flashed across the field,
How Peirse was never known to yield,
   She tells in stirring lays:
She tells in frightened periods
How Ridley's steps disturbed the infernal gods.
But hold! my muse is running wild
   On this too stirring theme:
It was her weakness from a child;
Excuse it, gentle reader, pray,
Now from her eyes I dare to say
   Prophetic flashes gleam.

Put not, rash man, thy hopes in all
Who can pursue the flying ball:
Not all of these shall dare to run
When fate reserves the prize for one:
Or if it shall most kindly be
Can never favour more than three.
Not all that I have named shall strive
The deadly struggle to survive:
Smith may despise all worldly pelf,
Start others but not start himself;
And Chitty may be turned reporter
In Hundred, hurdle race and Quarter,
And with his note-book scour the plain
With Chronicle upon the brain.
Yet some will start: and now we reach
The wisdom I design to teach:
My task I quickly will dispose of,
There are but three your prophet knows of
Who may be safely backed for places
In this, the shortest of the races,
Macaulay, Lawrence, Elliot these
Are they: the order if you please
I'll leave to you, and so remain
Yours truly till we meet again,
Poeta Etonensis qui
Stipendium meret Chronicli.

The Irish Vote

I would not swap my Irish Vote
  For a sight of the blind old Chian Bard;
I would not swap my Irish Vote
  For the satrapy of Scotland Yard.
For howsoe'er I trim and tack,
  My chance of power's not worth a groat,
Unless I pack behind my back
  An overwhelming Irish Vote.

Oh! what would be this House to me,
  Now John and Joseph stand aloof,
Without the sounds of Celtic glee
  That nightly ring beneath its roof?

I love the rich melodious brogue
  That ripples from Tim Healy's throat:
Oh! Tanner's an enchanting rogue,
  On whom I delicately dote.

My Irish Vote is staunch as steel,
  It never disobeys its head,
It shows no charity to Peel,
  But it has fearless faith *instead*.
It groans, it interrupts, it boos,
  It mocks the cock, the billy-goat;
But when *I* rise, no cushat coos
  More softly than my Irish Vote.

For Cromwell's crimes to weep I'm fain,
    Bodyke goes through me like a dart,
I've got Boyne Water on the brain,
    And Mitchelstown upon the heart.
I've bought a suit of Blarney tweed,
    And Blunt has lent me his top-coat;
Job's comforters no more I need,
    Enveloped in my Irish Vote.

I would not give my Irish Vote
    For Vanderbilt's portentous pile,
I'd yield without one murm'ring note
    A spring of everlasting ile.
In other days, when half a Tory,
    I stroked the old Coercion boat;
But now my only chance of glory
    Is centred in the Irish Vote.

The Last Ride together

after Robert Browning
(*From Her point of view*)

When I had firmly answered "No,"
And he allowed that that was so,
I really thought I should be free
For good and all from Mr B.,
   And that he would soberly acquiesce:
I said that it would be discreet
That for a while we should not meet;
I promised I would always feel
A kindly interest in his weal;
I thanked him for his amorous zeal;
   In short, I said all I could but "yes."

I said what I'm accustomed to;
I acted as I always do;
I promised he should find in me
A friend,—a sister, if that might be:
   But he was still dissatisfied:
He certainly was most polite;
He said exactly what was right,
He acted very properly,
Except indeed for this, that he
Insisted on inviting me
   To come with him for "one more last ride."

A little while in doubt I stood:
A ride, no doubt, would do me good:
I had a habit and a hat
Extremely well worth looking at:
    The weather was distinctly fine:
My horse too wanted exercise,
And time, when one is riding, flies:
Besides it really seemed, you see,
The only way of ridding me
Of pertinacious Mr B.:
    So my head I graciously incline.

I won't say much of what happened next:
I own I was extremely vexed:
Indeed I should have been aghast
If any one had seen what passed:
    But nobody need ever know
That, as I leaned forward to stir the fire,
He advanced before I could well retire,
And I suddenly felt, to my great alarm,
The grasp of a warm unlicensed arm,
An embrace in which I found no charm;
    I was awfully glad when he let me go.

Then we began to ride: my steed
Was rather fresh, too fresh indeed,
And at first I thought of little, save
The way to escape an early grave,
    As the dust rose up on either side.
My stern companion jogged along
On a brown old cob both broad and strong:
He looked as he does when he's writing verse,
Or endeavouring not to swear and curse,
Or wondering where he has left his purse:
    Indeed it was a sombre ride.

I spoke of the weather to Mr B.:
But he neither listened nor spoke to me:
I praised his horse, and I smiled the smile
Which was wont to move him once on a while;
    I said I was wearing his favourite flowers:
But I wasted my words on the desert air,
For he rode with a fixed and gloomy stare:
I wonder what he was thinking about:
As I don't read verse, I shan't find out:
It was something subtle and deep, no doubt,
    A theme to detain a man for hours.

Ah! there was the corner where Mr S.
So nearly induced me to whisper "yes":
And here it was that the next but one
Proposed on horseback, or would have done,
    Had his horse not most opportunely shied:
Which perhaps was due to the unseen flick
He received from my whip: 'twas a scurvy trick,
But I never could do with that young man:
I hope his present young woman can.
Well, I must say, never, since time began,
    Did I go for a duller or longer ride.

He never smiles and he never speaks:
He might go on like this for weeks:
He rolls a slightly frenzied eye
Towards the blue and burning sky,
    And the cob bounds on with tireless stride.
If we aren't at home for lunch at two
I don't know what Papa will do;
But I know full well he will say to me
"I never approved of Mr B.:
"It's the very devil that you and he
    "Ride, ride together, for ever ride."

The Literary and Scientific Society

after Arthur H. Clough

O ye musical nine, who drink the Castalian waters,
Seated on peaks of Olympus (or, if ye prefer it,
  Olumpos,—
Browning's a far better judge of the matter than
  yours very truly—),
Pray be so good as to give me assistance,—for,
  tho' I'm a poet,
I should be glad to receive a certain amount of
  assistance—,
Give me your help while I sing how SMITH, on the
  4th of December,
Did us the honour to read a paper entitled
  "Pompeii,"
In a Society whose name defies the restriction of
  metre.

Scarce need we tell of his fervour, research,
  erudition and learning,
These we must all have observed for ourselves, or at
  all events heard of,
Heard of from President PASHLEY, our eloquent
  President PASHLEY,

—Please to observe the effect of a skilfully cooked
    repetition,
Copied from Homer and Clough and a host of
    hexameter heroes;
Nor will we trouble our readers with all the parti-
    culars,—pictures,
Writings on walls and the like: but this we will
    say, that Sir Walter,
G. P. R. James and Lord Lytton must yield him
    the palm in description.
When he described how a skeleton dove had been
    found at Pompeii,
Found on a skeleton egg, we all of us wept in a
    chorus.

When he had done, and the weepers had wept,
    and the stamping was over,
PASHLEY arose, and he made some remarks in the
    usual fashion;
"This was an excellent paper, he seldom had heard
    such a good one,
"Yet there was one little thing he should like to
    make just one remark on,
"One little point where he did not agree with the
    reader's opinion,
"One little question on which Mr SMITH should
    have scarcely been silent":
Several more little points, and several more little
    questions,

148

Several more little things and so on and so on
  and so on;
Not that I wish to deny that his speech was exceedingly clever,
Or that we all of us paid him the greatest and
  deepest attention.
He was immediately followed by TATHAM (N.B. to
  the printer;
Do not omit to put all proper names in capital
  letters,
Partly because it looks well and smacks of the
  penny-a-liner,
Partly to comfort our friends when we cannot
  afford them a Mr):
Much information he gave concerning a building
  he'd heard of,
Five were its doors and its size 250×80.
JONES was the next to arise; and he made us a
  crushing oration,
Crushing, but pointless withal, like a seventy-ton
  steam hammer,
(Study that last line well, observe the onomatopoeia),
Crushed Mr SMITH with a hint that he had not
  neglected his Bulwer.

Then Mr WAYTE held forth, and his eloquence
    vied with his learning;
Oh for the tongue, or the pen or the pencil or
    something of some one,
Some one of fame, who was known from his youth
    as a friend of the Muses,
Then I might try to depict what was really the
    speech of the evening.
Now it is useless to try: we will only repeat his
    suggestion;—
If to Pompeii you go, be sure that you go on a
    Sunday.

Last Mr SHUCKBURGH spoke, and his speech was
    extremely delightful,
Touching on books and the like: we wish we had
    time to report it.

The Littlego

(Air: *Kaphoozelum*)

When I was young and wholly free
From any vice, however nice,
And did not yet aspire to be
Where men of beer and skittle go,
My young idea used to shoot,
Secure and gay, from day to day,
Until I met that hideous brute
The fiend-descended Littlego.

Chorus

Oh! the Littlego, the Littlego, the Littlego!
Oh! the Littlego, the daughter of the Devil!

Alas, poor victims that we are,
Who sport beside the Cam's clear tide,
Before we get us to the Bar,
To church or to Hospital go,
We study Mr Paley's views,
We have to deal with yards of steel,
We likewise woo the tragic muse,
And all to pass the Littlego.

Chorus

I too, like other men, was coached,
   Was duly packed with fact on fact,
And then that awful hall approached
   Where all who live by victual go:
They ploughed me once, they ploughed me twice,
   I won't say when those cruel men
Desisted, but let this suffice:
   I *did* get through the Littlego.

Chorus

I feel inclined to prophesy
   That this effete and obsolete
And hydra-headed pest will die
   And to perdition it 'll go:
They'll substitute for complex plans
   Incontinent abolishment,
And only antiquarians
   Will care about the Littlego.

Chorus

But still at that appalling hour
   When churchyards gape, a hideous shape
Behind me moved, by unseen power,
   Like some debauched bandit, 'ill go:
Enveloped in a Paley sheet,
   It waves on high an $x + y$,
And dogs me down each dismal street—
   The spectre of the Littlego.

Chorus

The Malefactor's Plea

Of sentences that stir my bile,
   Of phrases I detest,
There's one beyond all others vile;
   "He did it for the best."

Of course he did: I don't suppose,
   Nor can you think I should,
The man's among my deadliest foes,
   Or is not fairly good.

Of course he did it for the best:
   What should he do it for?
But did he do it? that's the test:
   I ask to know no more.

Alas! he did: and here am I,
   Quite ruined, half disgraced;
And you can really ask me why
   My wrath is not effaced:

And there is he, good worthy man,
   With self-esteem possessed,
Still saying, as of course, he can,
   "I did it for the best."

No evil deed was ever done,
   Or honest man withstood,
Since first this weary world begun,
   Except for some one's good.

And can it signify to me
    Whose good he did it for?
Mine was it? thus 'twas wont to be,
    And will be ever more.

When inoffensive people plant
    A dagger in your breast,
Your good is what they really want:
    They do it for the best.

The Old School List

In a wild moraine of forgotten books,
    On the glacier of years gone by,
As I plied my rake for order's sake,
    There was one that caught my eye:
And I sat by the shelf till I lost myself.
    And roamed in a crowded mist,
And heard lost voices and saw lost looks,
    As I pored on an Old School List.

What a jumble of names! there were some that I
        knew,
    As a brother is known: to-day
Gone I know not where, nay I hardly care,
    For their places are full: and, they—
What climes they have ranged: how much they're
        changed!
    Time, place and pursuits assist
In transforming them: stay where you are: adieu!
    You are all in the Old School List.

There are some who did nothing at school, much since:
    And others much then, since naught:
They are middle-aged men, grown bald since then:
    Some have travelled, and some have fought:
And some have written, and some are bitten
    With strange new faiths: desist
From tracking them: broker or priest or prince,
    They are all in the Old School List.

There's a grave grey lawyer in King's Bench Walk,
    Whose clients are passing few:
He seldom speaks: in those lonely weeks,
    What on earth can he find to do?
Well, he stroked the eight—what a splendid fate!—
    And the Newcastle barely missed:
"A future Lord Chancellor!" so we'd talk
    In the days of the old School List.

There were several duffers and several bores,
    Whose faces I've half forgot,
Whom I lived among, when the world was young,
    And who talked "no end of rot":
Are they now little clerks who stroll in the Parks
    Or scribble with grimy fist,
Or rich little peers who hire Scotch moors?
    Well—they're all in the old School List.

There were some who were certain to prosper and
      thrive,
    And certain to do no more,
Who were "capital chaps," and, tho' moderate *saps*,
    Would never stay in *after four:*
Now day after day they are packed away,
    After being connubially kissed,
To work in the city from ten to five:
    There they are in the old School List.

There were two good fellows I used to know.
   —How distant it all appears!
We played together in football weather,
   And messed together for years:
Now one of them's wed, and the other's dead
   So long that he's hardly missed
Save by us, who messed with him years ago:
   But we're all in the Old School List.

The Philosopher and the Philanthropist

Searching an infinite Where,
Probing a bottomless When,
   Dreamfully wandering,
   Ceaselessly pondering,
What is the Wherefore of men:
Bartering life for a There,
Selling his soul for a Then,
   Baffling obscurity,
   Conning futurity,
Usefulest, wisest of men!

Grasping the Present of Life,
Seizing a definite Now,
   Labouring thornfully,
   Banishing scornfully
Doubts of his Whither and How:
Spending his substance in Strife,
Working a practical How,
   Letting obscurity
   Rest on futurity,
Usefuler, wiser, I trow.

The Poet's Prayer

To buy my book—if you will be so kind—
   Is all I ask of you; and not to look
What fruit lies hid beneath the azure rind:
                To *buy* my book.

This for her hymn-book *Rosalind* mistook,
   When worshipping with yokel, maid, and hind;
Neaera read it in a flowery nook,
   And gave her loose curls to the wanton wind.
For this her grammar *Sylvia* once forsook,
   Of you I only ask—you will not mind?—
                To *buy* my book.

The Splinter

*Where's the philosopher can bear the toothache
patiently?*

One stormy day in winter,
   When all the world was snow,
I chanced upon a splinter,
   Which ran into my toe.
The world went round:
The stubborn ground
   Defied the deadliest dinter:
They brought me tea,
And muffins three:
My little maid
Fetched marmalade:
My grace I said,
And breakfasted:
But all that morn in winter
I thought about the splinter.

At ten o'clock
The postman's knock:
A friend was dead:
Another wed:
Two invitations:
Five objurgations:

A screed from my solicitor:
They brought the *Times:*
A list of crimes:
A deadly fight
'Twixt black and white:
A note from "B"
On Mr. G.,
And other things
From cats to Kings,
Known to that grand Inquisitor:—
But all that morn in winter,
I thought about the splinter.

But, oh; at last
A lady passed
   Beside my chamber casement,
With modest guise
And down-cast eyes
   And fair beyond amazement:
She passed away
Like some bright fay
   Too fair for earthly regions,
So sweet a sight
Would put to flight
   The fiend and all his legions!
And I, that noon in winter,
Forgot the cruel splinter.

The Street Organs Bill, 1891

Grinder, who serenely grindest,
  As thou groundest ages back,
Till thou ultimately findest
  Legislators on thy track:

Grinder, there is one Jacoby,
  There is Lubbock, prince of Barts,
Sternest of Professors: oh be-
  Ware of his infernal arts.

Guyer Hunter backed it boldly,
  Backed the Bart's oppressive bill:
So did he whose name is Staveley,
  And whose other name is Hill.

If they pass their cruel measure,
  If the House is true to them,
You must never give us pleasure,
  Grinder, after 8 p.m.

When the dawn with rosy finger,
  Dissipates the eastern gloom,
You and your machine must linger
  Silent in your silent room.

Grinder, if you are not willing,
    When invited, to desist,
You must pay your fortieth shilling,
    Wretched instrumentalist!

Failing that,—a fate unkinder—
    You must languish in a gaol
One laborious fortnight: grinder,
    Pray, oh pray that they may fail.

The Union of Hearts

What boots it, dissentient battalions,
    Of your birth and your breeding to brag,
To label us ragged rapscallions,
    Needy knights of the green carpet-bag?
Though fools by fine feathers be flattered,
    Snobs snared by Society's arts,
The Union of Caste shall be shattered
    By the Union of Hearts.

Girt around by your Stars and your Garters,
    Pert plant-bedding props of the Pale,
Ye rudely ride over our charters,
    Ye lock up our leaders in gaol.
Mad Marquis, your vessel, dismasted,
    Drifts to doom without compass or charts,
For the Union of Rank shall be blasted
    By the Union of Hearts.

Ye have millionaires rolling in riches,
    Ye count on the clan of the Guelph.
Whilst our champions are robbed of their breeches
    And poorly provided with pelf.
Yet muster the minions of Mammon,
    Make the most of the monarchs of marts,
For the Union of Gold is all gammon
    To the Union of Hearts.

We own that your speeches are spicy,
   We do not disparage your wit,
We envy your Lecky and Dicev,
   And Joseph resigned to his Pitt;
Your learning is deep and undoubted,
   Ye are men of remarkable parts,
But the Union of Heads shall be routed
   By the Union of Hearts.

Then avaunt, ye Coercionist croakers,
   For staunch and unshaken remains
The Alliance of Porridge and Pokers,
   Against the asssemblage of Brains.
Our flag no surrender shall sully,
   No shield stay our death-dealing darts,
For our war-cries are "Tanner and Tully!"
   And "The Union of Hearts!"

Time's Revenges

She broke my heart, as women do:
    Harm to harm-doers oft recurs;
It happened, in a year or two,
    That I broke hers.

To A. C. B.*

"What means this silence? Is't a seemly thing
Thus to provoke a friendly elder's ire?
Take notice then, that if thou answerest not,
A second letter follows close on this,
Third close on second, fourth as close on third,
And angry postcards rain as thick as hail
That slew Egyptia's cattle . . ."

*Arthur C. Benson

To a Friend

Whene'er I wander through the well-known fields,
Or guide my boat down the familiar stream,
And taste the joys which recollection yields,
When youth's delights are but a fading dream,
Where Windsor's keep his hoary head doth lift,
I'll think upon your gift.

And when you have occasion to refer
To Mr Browning's justly famous verses,
A thing which may from time to time occur,
To save one's giving vent to tears and curses,
(Although you may not catch the poet's drift)
You'll think upon my gift.

To A. H. C.*

(*In recollection of certain debates on the futility of Metaphysics*)

You taunt me as a shallow man:
　　You mock my prosy middle age:
Would demonstrate me, if you can,
　　Devoid of youth's exalted rage
　　Bound on a dusty pilgrimage.

Because I do not much peruse
　　The words that Schopenhauer penned;
Locke's, Kant's and Hegel's lofty views
　　I don't aspire to comprehend;
　　Because, in short, my worthy friend,

I'm, like yourself, a man of prose:
　　A man of commonplace belief,
Who doubts, and disbelieves, and knows,
　　And aims at joy, and flies from grief,
　　And has a taste for beer and beef.

You do us wrong: for you and I
　　Are just as good as other men:
A hand to write, a seeing eye,
　　An ear which catches, now and then,
　　The sounds that haunt a poet's pen:

*Arthur H. Clough

I offer (you withhold them) thanks
    For these, and other common things:
And not in vain on Cam's green banks
    We lived at Trinity and King's,
    And loved to try our sprouting wings.

A many-windowed house is life,
    And out of every window we,
In intervals of daily strife,
    Look forth upon infinity:
    And that's the good of you and me.

The joys of metaphysic trance,
    The midnight bliss of keen debate,
The insight of a mystic's glance,
    Which charm the undergraduate,
    Are matched in our maturer state.

The deeds and passions of our prime,
    Our studies of acknowledged truth,
Our business—though it's not sublime,—
    Are just as excellent in sooth,
    As all the fervour lost with youth.

The ruddy warmth of arduous toil,
    The spasm of triumphant strife,
A friend to serve, a foe to foil,
    A cause with noble purpose rife,
    The love of her that gave thee life:

The smile that shines through misty tears,
    The soft "delight of low replies,"
The after-glow of vanished fears,
      And all the excellent surprise
      That trembles in a woman's eyes:

Men, women, children: speech and song:
    The artist's touch, the poet's thought:
The pulses of a busy throng,
      The rest of spirits over-wrought:
      Are these—is all beside them, naught?

Here, everywhere, and every day,
    The seeker finds right human stuff:
To laugh, to weep, to work, to play;
      Are joy and sorrow not enough?
      And cannot these content thee, Clough?

To a Lady

A pipe's a merry madrigal,
   A stately sonnet a cigar,
The homely clay at close of day
   A stanza to the evening star,
The cigarette a canzonette
   Both amorous and musical.

But as the song requires a tune,
   A madrigal must aptly rhyme,
A sonnet shines in measured lines,
   Each foot must walk in proper time,
And music's aid is best displayed
   When duly matched with verses fair:

So sweetest meerschaum needs a case,
   Cigars are clipped with dainty blade,
The seasoned briar will still aspire
   To lights in silvern casket laid,
The cigarette is duly set
   In holder rich with every grace.

And every cigarette consumed
   Is fragrant homage offered thee;
The mellow streak, from week to week,
   Embrowns thy gift bestowed on me:—
So every hour proclaims the power
   Of her whose gift the smoke perfumes.

To an Indiscreet Critic

As J. K. S. I made my bid for fame
   And money, which is sweeter than success,
Though Mr —— is possibly the same
                  as J. K. S.

Was it perhaps an *error of the press*?
   Is some malign *compositor* to blame?
Or was it just the *reader's* carelessness?
   Or your astute *reviewer's* little game,—
His *lapsus calami* as I should guess?
   In any case I wish to sign my name
                  as J. K. S.

To a Rejected Lover

Friend, why so gloomy? why so glum?
   Why such a dull lack-lustre eye?
At festive meetings why so dumb?
   From dearest friend so apt to fly?
You must have got a reason: come!

I know she's young, I know she's fair;
   I know she's beautiful and sweet:
I know her wealth of golden hair,
   Her sunny eyes, her tiny feet;
I do not bid you not despair

Of ever being more to her
   Than half a dozen other men:
She's going, if I do not err
   To marry some one else: what then?
I see no cause for such a stir.

It isn't what one *hasn't got*
   That ought to quench the light of life:
It's what one *loses:* is it not?
   It's death, or treason in a wife:
It's finding one's unhappy lot

Comprises foes, and friends untrue,
   Grief, worry, sickness, even crime:
And I should only pity you,
   If aught of these should come with time:
Not blame you as I own I do.

You haven't got a thousand pounds:
   You cannot write yourself M.P.:
There are not any solid grounds
   For thinking you will ever be
A very famous man: but, zounds!

You don't, on that account, exclaim
   That life's a curse, or birth a blight,
Nor do you minimise, or blame,
   Such merits as are yours by right:
Well, be your conduct still the same!

From what you haven't gaily turn
   To what you have: the world's alive:
Still pulses beat, still passions burn:
   There's still to work, there's still to strive:
The curse is easy to discern.

I do not bid you to forget,
   Nor say that she is full of flaws,
Nor rail on womankind: nor yet
   Bestow a meed of just applause
On Amabel, or Violet:

Nor say the sea is full of fish
   As good as those which others catch:
Indeed I do not greatly wish
   To urge you to another match:
I only say that life's a dish

Well worth the eating, even when
   You cannot get the sauce you like;
You have a pair of hands, a pen,
   A tongue: I've seen you work, and strike
A blow worth striking now and then.

So don't be gloomy, don't be glum,
   Nor give a thought to what you lack:
Take what you have: no longer dumb
   Nor idle; hit misfortune back,
And own that I have reason: come!

To A. S.*

after Robert Browning

Birthdays? yes, in a general way;
For the most if not for the best of men:
You were born (I suppose) on a certain day:
So was I: or perhaps in the night: what then?

Only this: or at least, if more,
You must know, not think it, and learn, not speak:
There is truth to be found on the unknown shore,
And many will find where few will seek.

For many are called and few are chosen,
And the few grow many as ages lapse:
But when will the many grow few: what dozen
Is fused into one by Time's hammer-taps?

A bare brown stone in a babbling brook:—
It was wanton to hurl it there, you say:
And the moss, which clung in the sheltered nook
(Yet the stream runs cooler), is washed away.

That begs the question: many a prater
Thinks such a suggestion a sound "stop thief!"
Which, may I ask, do you think the greater,
Sergeant-at-arms or a Robber Chief?

*Archibald Smith

And if it were not so? still you doubt?
Ah! yours is a birthday indeed if so.
That were something to write a poem about,
If one thought a little. I only know.

P.S.

There's a Me Society down at Cambridge,
Where my works, *cum notis variorum*,
Are talked about; well, I require the same bridge
That Euclid took toll as at *Asinorum:*

And, as they have got through several ditties
I thought were as stiff as a brick-built wall,
I've composed the above, and a stiff one *it* is,
A bridge to stop asses at, once for all.

To B. H. H*

(On his travels)

And will thy travels never end?
And wilt thou not return, my friend?
Shall Piccadilly never more,
Amid the busses' daily roar,
Where prowls the Baron's stately goat,
Thy philosophic footfall note?
Nor ever will the Savile's board
The dainties of the hour afford
To one grave form amid the Babel
Which girds that lofty-minded table?

Come: for we miss thee. That slow smile
Has failed us now too long a while:
That network of ingenious phrase
Suggesting more than what it says:
The literary epigram
Which gracefully unmasks a sham,
Or else awards judicious praise
To one who earns but wears not bays,
Are lacking in our midst, and we
Drift, rudderless, about a sea
Of conversation unadorned
By him whose absence long we've mourned.

*Bernard H. Holland

Come: for *I* need you: more or less
Because I love to play at chess;
Partly because I want to know
Your views about a book or so,
Which I have published, or intend
To publish: most of all, my friend,
Because I found thy converse sweet,
Thy fellowship a joy complete,
And life is short and art is long,
And still the absent suffer wrong.

I know not where thy footsteps stray,
Nor what the ordering of thy day:
If now thy graceful shallop slips
Amid the gorgeous Eastern ships,
Where some vast river makes a lane
Across the forest-hidden plain:
If, stretched upon a soft divan,
You lounge, as orientals can,
And trace the rings of fragrant smoke
One graceful moment soar unbroke;
While, lo, the wordless Kitmagar
Presents the welcome waterjar,
And swart Chuprassis stand at ease,
Beneath umbrageous banyan trees:
If now perchance the crescent moon
Hangs high, at night's reposeful noon,
Against a gloomy purple sky,
Star-studded in its majesty,
While slow you walk alone, and deep
In thoughts that bring more rest than sleep.

Come, anyhow: if not to find
An occupation to thy mind,
Nor yet a Fortunatus' purse,
Nor any cure for any curse:
Come, talk, live, marry, work, write, sing;
Be eloquent on anything:
Be active in whatever line:
And if a sun less splendid shine,
And vegetation less profuse,
And persons worthier of abuse,
Are found with us than now with you;
Still, though our merits may be few,
We are at least thy friends of youth,
Thy fellow-seekers after truth,
Thy fellow-talkers, fellow-bards,
Thy fellows still in all regards;
So turn again towards the West,
And grasp their hands who love you best.

To C. S. C.*

Oh, when the grey courts of Christ's College glowed
With all the rapture of thy frequent lay,
When printers' devils chuckled as they strode,
And blithe compositors grew loudly gay:
Did Granta realise that here abode,
Here in the home of Milton, Wordsworth, Gray,
A poet not unfit to cope with any
That ever wore the bays or turned a penny?

The wit of smooth delicious Matthew Prior,
The rhythmic grace which Hookham Frere displayed,
The summer lightning wreathing Byron's lyre,
The neat inevitable turns of Praed,
Rhymes to which Hudibras could scarce aspire,
Such metric pranks as Gilbert oft has played,
All these good gifts and others far sublimer
Are found in thee, beloved Cambridge rhymer.

And scholarship as sound as his whose name
Matched thine (he lives to mourn, alas, thy death,
And now enjoys the plenitude of fame,
And oft to crowded audience lectureth,
Or writes to prove religion is the same
As science, unbelief a form of faith):–
Ripe scholar! Virgil's self would not be chary
Of praises for thy *Carmen Seculare*.

*Charles S. Calverley

Whene'er I take my "pint of beer" a day,
I "gaze into my glass" and think of thee:
When smoking, after "lunch is cleared away,"
Thy face amid the cloud I seem to see;
When "that sweet mite with whom I used to play,"
Or "Araminta," or "the fair Miss P."
Recur to me, I think upon thy verses,
Which still my beating heart and quench my curses.

Ah, Calverley! if in these lays of mine
Some sparkle of thy radiant genius burned,
Or were in any poem—stanza—line
Some faint reflection of thy muse discerned:
If any critic would remark in fine
"Of C. S. C. this gentle art he learned;"
I should not then expect my book to fail,
Nor have my doubts about a decent sale.

To Mrs B.

The sumptuous board of you know who
   Was rich with unaccustomed splendour:
The host, a gallant man and true,
   Beamed like a newly polished fender:
And more than one important guest
   With visible delight was swelling:
But that which I remember best
   Is just a phrase:— "How's Helen?"

I sat, a melancholy man,
   Beside a newly-married lady,
And wondered how, if I began,
   To shun the trivial, dull and shady;
When through the dinner-din I caught
   A question I remember well, in
My hours of retrospective thought:
   My neighbour said:— "How's Helen?"

I do not know how Helen was:
   —She's almost always doing fairly—:
Nor do I greatly care, because
   The question, which was asked so squarely,
Produced an excellent effect
   Both then and since: it's truth I'm telling;
And that is why I recollect
   The simple phrase: "How's Helen?"

To my Friend's Wife

(*reading Murray's Magazine*)

Men talk, men work, men glow, men live, men die,
　　Peal at the ear and lighten in the eye:
While woman, wedded to a magazine,
　　Turns one cold eye upon the maddening scene.

To My Readers

I do not boast a poet's bays,
  Nor claim to wield a poet's pen,
Nor do I hope for many days
  To buzz about the mouths of men.

I claim to be the sort of man
  Who studies metrical effect:
Whose verse generally scan:
  Whose rhymes are commonly correct;

And when I chance upon a thought
  Which seems to shape itself in rhyme,
I like to treat it as I ought,
  Unless the theme be too sublime.

It may be pleasure to rehearse,
  When twilight deepens out of day,
The tinkle of a tiny verse
  Which wiled the noon-tide hours away.

It may be pleasure to recall
  The friends of yesterday to-morrow
But that's a pleasure—if at all—
  Which borders very near on sorrow.

So, if I try to make you laugh,
   Or if I chance to make you weep,
Your comrade when you crunch and quaff,
   Your solace when you cannot sleep.

Its merely as a common man
   Who says what other people say,
And hopes to end as he began,
   A treader of the beaten way.

To One that Smokes

after Frederic W. H. Myers

Spare us the hint of slightest desecration,
　　Spotless preserve us an untainted shrine;
Not for thy sake, oh goddess of creation,
　　Not for thy sake, oh woman, but for mine.

To P. L., aged 4½

Ah Phyllis! did I only dare
  To hope that, as the years go by,
And you, a maid divinely fair,
  The cynosure of every eye,
Have fixed the wandering minds of men,
  And found a fare for scores of hearses,
You still will open, now and then,
  My little book of verses;

Or did I, bolder yet, aspire
  To hope that any phrase of mine,
Aglow with memory's cheering fire
  Will burn within that heart of thine;
Although my brow be bare of bays,
  My coffers not replete with gain,
I shall not—what's the foolish phrase?—
  Have written quite in vain.

To R. K.*

As long I dwell on some stupendous
And tremendous (Heaven defend us!)
Monstr'-inform'-ingens-horrendous
Demoniaco-seraphic
Penman's latest piece of graphic.

Browning

Will there never come a season
Which shall rid us from the curse
Of a prose which knows no reason
And an unmelodious verse:
When the world shall cease to wonder
At the genius of an Ass,
And a boy's eccentric blunder
Shall not bring success to pass:

When mankind shall be delivered
From the clash of magazines,
And the inkstand shall be shivered
Into countless smithereens:
When there stands a muzzled stripling,
Mute, beside a muzzled bore:
When the Rudyards cease from kipling
And the Haggards Ride no more.

*Rudyard Kipling

To Simeon Stylites

I will not pay you, sir, for candid criticism,
    But I will print it, if it comes this way;
Though every paragraph enshrines a witticism,
                          I will not pay.

Send me a letter, Simeon, every day,
    Blame every ugly heresy or pretty schism:
All have their critics; look at Mr. A.:
    I own that I—whereas he says he pities his - am
Disposed to honour mine: go on, then, pray:
    Multiply words which end in (good Stylites!) "ism":
                          I will not pay.

P.S.—What? No more rhymes, dear Simeon?
                         Wait a bit: I see some;
A maid once said—her way she had forgot—
    "London is twice as big as other cities is, 'm."
                          What?

Dublin's Lord Mayor has done what he should not.
    But need you punish for his crime (if it is his) him?
He has, you know, like others of the lot,
    A strong belief in Parnell - (see his Ditties) ism:
The man, confound him, is a patriot:
    Has principles as Fox or Mr. Pitt has his : h'm!
                          What?

To W. H.*

What are the habits of the ruby flood
We reek with? man had questioned many a year:
And William Harvey spoke in accents clear
These words: "the circulation of the blood."
Man owned that this was so, and asked for food;
And fate bestowed upon him beef and beer:
But beef was coarse, indelicate and sere:
So Harvey proffered Sauce and made it good.
My friend! be worthy of thy forbears' glory,
And if old truths thou canst not rediscover,
Yet canst thou live those truths out here on earth:
Make stagnant conversations, void of mirth,
To circulate with quip and crank and story,
Make life's dull dish with piquant sauce run over.

*Walter Headlam

Written on the Fly-Leaf of Maclise's Portrait Gallery, Edited by Bates

Here, painted by a Master's hand,
   Is many a lovely dame,
Amidst the writers of the land
   Who gained the greatest fame.

But sure there is not one whose pen
   Was half so apt as thine
To catch the ears of listening men,
   Or wake the Sacred Nine.

None saw reflected in her glass
   A more distinguished face:
But thou art born too late, alas!
   To take thy proper place.

The pencil of Maclise, my dear,
   Thy face will ne'er portray,
Nor will the facts of thy career
   Be told by Bates, B.A.

Yet do not hence a pretext seize
   To blame the cruel Fates:
If they denied thee to Maclise,
   They rescued thee from Bates.

Written on the Fly-Leaf of Treasure Island by a "Hesitating Purchaser."

It sounds magnificent: but then
 Perhaps I am a little old,
To buy a tale of lawless men,
 Who scuttle ships and bury gold.

Yet still I love a pirate crew,
 Still dote upon a buccaneer;
I'll buy the book, and read it through,
 And pass it on to you, my dear.

Farewell! I've other work to do:

Another way of reaching men

But I shall still remember you

You've served me well! adieu, dear Pen!

JKS 1891